ASIA PACIFIC SECURITY OUTLOOK 1998

The cosponsors of this project wish to thank

APAP
Asia Pacific Agenda Project

The Nippon Foundation

ASIA PACIFIC SECURITY OUTLOOK
1998

edited by
Charles E. Morrison

cosponsored by
ASEAN Institutes for Strategic and International Studies
East-West Center
Japan Center for International Exchange

AN APAP PROJECT

JCIE

Tokyo • Japan Center for International Exchange • New York

Copyright © 1998 Japan Center for International Exchange
All rights reserved.

The surnames of the authors and other persons mentioned in this book are positioned according to country practice.

Copyediting by Pamela J. Noda.
Cover and typographic design by Becky Davis, EDS Inc.,
Editorial & Design Services. Typesetting and production by EDS Inc.

Printed in Japan.
ISBN 4-88907-015-x

Distributed worldwide outside Japan by Brookings Institution Press, 1775 Massachusetts Avenue, N.W., Washington, D.C. 20036-2188 U.S.A.

Japan Center for International Exchange
9-7 Minami Azabu 4-chome, Minato-ku, Tokyo 106-0047 Japan

URL: http://www.jcie.or.jp

Japan Center for International Exchange, Inc. (JCIE/USA)
1251 Avenue of the Americas, New York, N.Y. 10020 U.S.A.

Contents

Foreword 7
The Regional Overview 9

1. Australia 23
2. Canada 32
3. China 41
4. The European Union 50
5. Indonesia 58
6. Japan 65
7. Republic of Korea 77
8. Malaysia 86
9. New Zealand 92
10. Papua New Guinea 101
11. The Philippines 108
12. Russia 118
13. Singapore 129
14. Thailand 136
15. The United States 147
16. Vietnam 157

Foreword

The Japan Center for International Exchange (JCIE) is pleased to be the principal sponsor of the *Asia Pacific Security Outlook* as a project within the Asia Pacific Agenda Program (APAP). JCIE intends that the *Outlook,* of which the 1998 edition is the second issue, be a regular annual publication. We are grateful to our cosponsoring institutions, the ASEAN Institutes for Strategic and International Studies (ASEAN-ISIS) and the East-West Center, for their help in making this endeavor a success.

Like other APAP activities, the *Outlook* provides a venue for specialists from Asia Pacific to work together on important challenges facing the region. The *Outlook* seeks to contribute to the search for a new regional security order by monitoring changing perceptions of the security environment, national defense doctrines and issues, and contributions to regional and global security. We hope that this monitoring as well as the vigorous discussions and debate among the members of the *Outlook* analytical team will contribute to building a broader basis of understanding of each country's sensitivities as well as engendering a more realistic assessment of the prospects and challenges of building a new security order.

The *Outlook* team has multinational leadership and authorship from Asia Pacific itself. Its three directors are Charles E. Morrison (U.S.A.), Nishihara Masashi (Japan), and Jusuf Wanandi (Indonesia). The bulk of the work, however, falls on a team of security analysts from 16 countries, many of them younger specialists, each of whom wrote a background paper on his or her own country. In November 1997, these analysts came together at JCIE with the three project directors and other invited analysts to review and critique each other's papers and to discuss regional security issues in general. This discussion and a questionnaire filled out by the analysts help to inform the regional overview.

The *Outlook* is keyed to the ASEAN Regional Forum (ARF), a dialogue process initiated by the Association of Southeast Asian Nations in 1994. The countries covered in the *Outlook* are members of ARF, although the *Outlook* does not now cover all members. We regard the *Outlook* as a work in progress; over time, the coverage of issues and countries will expand and deepen.

JCIE is grateful to APAP and the Nippon Foundation for financial support of the *Asia Pacific Security Outlook 1998*. We also want to acknowledge the important role played by the Center for Global Partnership in sponsoring *Asia Pacific Security Outlook 1997*, which was published by the East-West Center. The editor joins me in expressing our gratitude to Richard W. Baker of the East-West Center for assistance at all stages of the editing process and to Clara Joewono of the Centre for Strategic and International Studies in Indonesia for coordinating inputs among the ASEAN-ISIS members.

Finally, I should note that JCIE seeks wide dissemination of the products associated with our program. Readers are invited to explore JCIE's website at <http://www.jcie.or.jp> for more information on APAP and other JCIE programs. We also welcome your suggestions for improving future editions of the *Asia Pacific Security Outlook*.

YAMAMOTO TADASHI
PRESIDENT
JAPAN CENTER FOR INTERNATIONAL EXCHANGE

The Regional Overview

At the beginning of 1998, the Asia Pacific security outlook presented two contrasting faces. International political relations among the major states were never better, providing the basis for a relatively optimistic outlook. Yet the region's worst economic crisis in decades threatened a traditional basis for security optimism: the Asian economic success story.

The dimensions of the financial crisis were still unfolding at the beginning of 1998, making hazardous any predictions about their full scope, depth, and duration. Throughout the latter half of 1997, governments, international organizations, and most mainstream economic analysis had consistently underestimated the seriousness of the crisis. International bailout programs in Indonesia, South Korea, and Thailand, designed to impress domestic and foreign investors, had failed to restore confidence. The region's governments increasingly concluded that even once market stability was achieved, the restoration of economic confidence and sound growth would come only after two, three, or even more years of substantial economic pain.

THE FINANCIAL CRISIS AS A SECURITY PROBLEM

In the minds of the analysts associated with the *Asia Pacific Security Outlook 1998,* the financial crisis is a serious security concern and should be added to the previous year's "watch list" issues: large power relations, the Korean peninsula, territorial disputes, and weapons procurement. It is frequently pointed out that many of the region's macroeconomic fundamentals remain strong—high savings, low inflation, and balanced government budgets. If, on the one hand, the affected countries are able to make appropriate changes in policies or practices and the world markets for capital and goods remain open to them, the region may reemerge from the crisis with a sounder base for sustained growth than before. On the other hand, the crisis could continue to spread as the result of a combination of policy failures and contagion, adjustments may not be made, or international support in the form of long-term capital availability or market access may not be adequate. If prolonged, the sudden downturn in the region's economic fortunes could have a devastating impact not only on individual lives and fortunes—that is, on individual or human security—but also on national politics, regime stability, and international relations. Three possible impacts are considered here.

Socioeconomic Discontent Threatening Domestic Stability. This is the greatest security challenge arising from the economic crisis. High growth in the past has increased expectations of economic performance, particularly among the young, and progress came relatively easily as changes in global competitiveness and open world markets favored many Asian economies. But the promise of higher living standards is now compromised as millions of East Asians face the loss of jobs and income. Unemployment and inflation rates are expected to rise steeply in 1998 to levels unprecedented in recent times in Indonesia, South Korea, and Thailand. The economic pain will increasingly affect the previously upwardly mobile middle and professional classes, key bases of political support in most Asian societies. Domestic political leadership or even political systems, many of which base their legitimacy on economic performance, will come under increased pressure. The governments with more flexible political systems appear to be in a better position to shift policies. But even for those governments whose legitimacy is based in part on noneconomic factors such as popular election, a prolonged crisis may result in growing disenchantment with the political system and a corresponding nostalgia for strongman leadership associated with better or at least improving times, such as those of Park Chung-hee in South Korea or Sarit Thanarit in Thailand.

Increased Tensions in Relations within Asia. These could arise from a number of factors. Anxieties and nationalism may rise in states that have suffered relative declines in their positions compared with their neighbors. Weakened leaders or governments may be tempted to blame outsiders or look for outside diversions to deflect domestic criticism. Expulsions of foreign workers at a time of reduced opportunities in their homelands could exacerbate tensions between host countries and sending countries. Internal ethnic tensions could spill over into international relationships or create waves of new refugees.

Increased Tensions between Asian Countries and the United States. In Asia, such tensions could arise over U.S. support for painful International Monetary Fund (IMF) austerity measures or American purchases of Asian assets at bargain prices, affronting nationalistic sentiments. In the United States, increased Asian trade surpluses, an inevitable short- and medium-term consequence of the crisis, could result in a severe backlash. Other sources of tension lie in Asian perceptions of a lack of U.S. support, a problem that is particularly acute in Thailand, and even suspicions that the United States engineered or at least welcomed the crisis to cut Asia down to size. In contrast, public perception in the United States is that American taxpayers are being asked to foot the bill to bail out profligate borrowers in Asia as well as Western commercial lenders who made unwise loans.

On the positive side, the financial crisis not only could result in basically strong future economies but also could stimulate strengthened regional cooperation. The crisis called attention to the close linkage among the Asian economies, and has resulted in contributions to the IMF packages for Indonesia, South Korea, and Thailand from those regional economies with stronger reserve positions, including Brunei, China, Japan, Malaysia, Singapore, and Taiwan. While global institutions rather than regional institutions have led the response, the Asia-Pacific Economic Cooperation (APEC) Leaders' Meeting in Vancouver in November 1997 agreed on enhanced monitoring and some kind of supplemental swapping arrangements, with details to be worked out. For the present, most of the implications of the financial crisis are on the downside, but in the longer run, lessons and new forms of cooperation drawn from the crisis could enhance the region's economic and security outlook.

THE 1997 WATCH LIST ISSUES

Turning to the 1997 watch list items, virtually all analysts saw a significant improvement in large power relations, marked by the change in Sino-American relations following the annual renewal in the summer by the United States of China's nondiscriminatory trade status.

Analyst opinion on whether there had been an improvement on the other issues—the Korean peninsula, territorial questions, and weapons proliferation—was more cautious. In all cases, there were noticeably fewer highly visible incidents or developments to attract public and media attention. Nevertheless, all watch list issues continue to bear close watching. Nothing has happened to the fundamentals of any of these issues that would reduce their potential danger to the regional security outlook.

LARGE POWER RELATIONS   The year 1997 was notable for its many bilateral meetings among leaders of the four largest countries of the region, China, Japan, Russia, and the United States, as each bilateral relationship improved simultaneously with the others. This was suggestive of the policy emphases of the large powers: China was active diplomatically, seeking improvements in its relations with neighbors on a broad front. Following the Denver Group of Eight summit in July, Japan took a strong interest in improving relations with Russia, its long-standing territorial grievances having hitherto constrained rapprochement. Russia's reemergence as a diplomatic player can be partly attributed to President Boris Yeltsin's physical recovery and partly to the long-awaited but still fragile stabilization of the Russian economy. U.S. President Bill Clinton, having, early in his presidency, adopted with little success a more confrontational approach to issues with the larger Asian powers, appeared anxious to avoid conflicts and to use positive approaches and personal diplomacy to achieve American goals in the region.

Of the bilateral activities, Chinese President Jiang Zemin's visit to the United States in late October received the most attention as it was the first state visit to Washington by a Chinese leader since the Tiananmen Square incident of 1989 and marked a significant shift in tone in what has been the most troubled bilateral large power relationship in recent years. In March 1996, American warships were sent to the vicinity of the Taiwan Strait during Chinese missile tests in the area. In 1997, however, the smooth handover of Hong Kong and the U.S. continuation of China's nondiscriminatory trade status helped smooth the way for the trip, as did the confirmation of Jiang's leadership position at the time of the 15th Party Congress in September. The trip was marked by an explicit statement of differences on some items and protest demonstrations in most of the cities Jiang visited, but the leaders were both determined to keep the tone of the trip positive and the

U.S. Congress was unusually cooperative. Although the results of the trip were more symbolic than substantive, China and the United States both made a number of important gestures, including the lifting of nuclear technology export controls on China by the United States and, after Jiang returned home, the release by China of dissident Wei Jingsheng, who went into exile in the United States. The tone of good feeling is expected to continue in 1998 as both sides prepare for a successful trip by Clinton to Beijing in midyear.

The Boris Yeltsin–Hashimoto Ryutaro "no necktie" summit at the beginning of November 1997 marked a significant shift in a hitherto cool Russian-Japanese relationship. The setting itself, in the Siberian city of Krasnoyarsk, approximately equidistant between Moscow and Tokyo, set a tone of compromise. In a pledge that demonstrated just how problematic and antiquated the relationship has been, the two leaders agreed to work toward a World War II peace agreement by the year 2000. In addition to economic agreements focusing on the development of Siberia and the Russian Far East, it was agreed to step up military exchanges. The long-standing territorial dispute, previously an obstacle to improved Russian-Japanese cooperation, was set aside for the time being.

The "strategic cooperative partnership" between Russia and China was highlighted by high-level visits, including Jiang's trip to Moscow in April and Yeltsin's to Beijing in November. The April visit resulted in a five-state agreement reducing military forces along the former Sino-Soviet border, and the November visit yielded a frontier demarcation treaty. During 1997, the two countries also agreed on economic cooperation projects, including a framework accord for building a US$12 billion gas pipeline from Siberia to Northeast China.

The one distinctly negative note in large power relations came in the form of Chinese objections to the new Guidelines for U.S.-Japan Defense Cooperation. This issue cast a slight shadow over Hashimoto's visit to Beijing in early September to celebrate the 25th anniversary of the normalization of Sino-Japanese diplomatic relations. The China, Japan, and U.S. chapters in this report set out these differences in national perceptions. The Chinese regard the guidelines as directed toward China, and particularly toward the Taiwan situation. The Japanese and Americans regard the guidelines as a logical outgrowth of their established alliance, which they believe to be beneficial to regional stability. They made a considerable effort to introduce transparency into the process of preparing the guidelines, setting out an interim report for comment before the final agreement was reached in September. Despite the differences in large power perceptions, the new guidelines did not lead to a crisis in relations. Indeed, Jiang's visit to Washington occurred about a month later with little reference to the bilateral U.S.-Japan Security Treaty, and Chinese Premier Li Peng visited Japan in November.

The Taiwan question remains the thorniest problem in China's relations with the United States and Japan. No incidents occurred in 1997 comparable to the Chinese missile tests in 1995 and 1996, and some minor steps improved cross-strait relations, including an opening of limited direct shipping as well as a resumption of semiofficial contacts at a relatively low level in April after a 22-month hiatus. Taiwanese authorities rejected Beijing's suggestions of the Hong Kong model of "one country, two systems" as a desirable formula for cross-strait reunification and continued to push to expand their political relations with other governments. Taiwan's military modernization, the local electoral successes of the more independence-minded opposition Democratic Progressive Party, and increased informal Taiwanese contacts with Asian leaders in the wake of the region's financial crisis are all matters of great sensitivity in Beijing. For the time being, however, officials in Beijing, Taipei, and Washington are exercising restraint in handling the delicate issues relating to future cross-strait relations.

The upsurge in bilateral initiatives among the larger powers reflects the fluid post–cold war environment. All the larger powers are seeking multiple relationships and none wants to be trapped into a permanent or semipermanent hostility. Some sources of tensions, notably ideology, have declined as a factor affecting international relations. This has provided a window of opportunity to build constructive dialogue across long-standing divides, as in the case of Russian-Japanese relations in 1997. But while flexibility and the willingness to engage in constructive dialogues are at an all-time high, suspicions of each other's motives linger beneath the surface. In most cases, truly strategic partnerships, to borrow a phrase used to describe the Russian-Chinese relationship and the aspiration for Sino-American relations, remain to be built, at both the grass-roots level and among the elites.

KOREAN PENINSULA   The Korean peninsula was also relatively free of incidents in 1997. An improved atmosphere was established by North Korea's January 10 expression of "deep regret" for the intrusion into South Korean waters of a coastal submarine in September

1996. Groundbreaking took place in August 1997 for preparation of the site for the light water reactors being delivered to North Korea under the auspices of the Korean Peninsula Energy Development Organization (KEDO), and after many stops and starts, Four-Party Talks to replace the 1953 armistice agreement finally commenced in Geneva in December 1997. Despite the severe food shortages in North Korea and increasing numbers of defections, most significantly high-level ideologue Hwang Jang Yop in February, the Kim Jong Il regime appeared to have fully consolidated its position, and talk of an early North Korean collapse died down. In South Korea, the severe economic crisis at the end of the year turned the country's attention to what for most South Korean citizens was a much more immediate problem.

Absent from the diplomacy surrounding the peninsula was any significant progress in North-South relations. There had been breakthroughs in the early 1990s, most particularly the promise of making the peninsula nuclear-free, verified by some form of bilateral inspections, but these came to naught after tensions arose over the North's nuclear program. The December 18, 1997, election of Kim Dae Jung as president of South Korea provided the country with a leader who may be more acceptable to the North as a dialogue partner. The economic crisis in South Korea, while in no way eliminating its huge economic lead over the North, may have had a sobering effect. In some respects, therefore, the environment for renewed North-South dialogue has been set, but it will still take leadership and a significant measure of political courage to get serious dialogue under way and on a productive course.

TERRITORIAL DISPUTES Territorial disputes are a watch list issue because they are so widespread and in certain circumstances can capture nationalist sentiments and flare up into important international disputes. In contrast to some recent years, there was little attention given in 1997 to the region's principal territorial disputes—the Northern Territories issue between Japan and Russia, the Tok Do/Takeshima Island involving South Korea and Japan, the Senkaku/Diaoyu Islands involving Japan and China, the Paracels involving China and Vietnam, and the Spratlys involving Brunei, China, the Philippines, Malaysia, and Vietnam.

Some incidents that occurred were the Chinese emplacement in March of an oil rig in waters off Hainan claimed by Vietnam, the

Philippine arrest of Chinese fishermen on Scarborough Reef in May, and some verbal sparring over Tok Do. These incidents were relatively self-contained. The paucity of incidents, however, should not be regarded as a particularly positive sign. Since governments have been politically unable to compromise their claims or have them adjudicated, they continue to fester, waiting for solution by the "next generation." As such, they remain time bombs for Asia's future that may be exploited in the future by governments or nationalistic activist groups for their own purposes.

WEAPONS PROCUREMENT   Virtually all defense forces in the Asia Pacific region are engaged in military modernization programs involving a significant upgrading of weapons systems. Our security analysts generally do not regard military modernization as a threat to regional stability, for several reasons. In most cases, modernization is not associated with any clear-cut enemy and thus does not have the character of an arms race. Also in most cases, defense effort measured as a share of gross national product has been declining. Moreover, weapons modernization is associated with declining manpower in virtually all countries. Finally, in many countries defense equipment has become obsolete and new missions, such as better policing of Exclusive Economic Zones, do require new purchases.

The economic crisis caused defense budget cuts and reduced the international purchasing power of many Asian governments, thus dampening the region's appetite for sophisticated new weapons systems. Possible domestic repercussions are increased conflict between defense ministries and other agencies to protect their budgets, and reduced military morale. International repercussions may include controversies with suppliers over existing contracts or well-advanced procurement commitments and efforts to switch sources to cheaper weapons suppliers such as Russia and China as opposed to the United States and Western Europe. The international purchasing power of the defense budgets of countries like China, whose currencies have been least affected by the economic crisis, will increase relative to those most affected.

Reduced weapons purchases will delay the ability of some of the region's armed forces to assume new missions. In many countries, new equipment purchases have been associated with a growing interest in naval and air capabilities. This suggests that the region's defense planners see modern contingencies as less likely to involve mass numbers of ground forces and more likely to require monitoring, patrolling, and rapid responses by more highly mobile forces. Such contingencies might involve, for example, the detection of illegal fishing, illegal migrants, or terrorists. Even in South Korea, which is the only member country of the ASEAN Regional Forum (ARF) to face large numbers of ground troops across a heavily armed border, there has been a new emphasis on maritime and air capabilities.

Other Regional Issues

INTERNAL CONFLICT   The potential for internal turmoil as a result of the financial crisis has been described. In reality, however, thus far internal conflict has remained at a relatively low ebb. Several weaker states within the region have chronic internal security problems, but in no case has the control of the central authorities been seriously threatened. Overall, the region's record in achieving reconciliation in internal conflict during 1997 was mixed. Positive strides were made in Papua New Guinea and in the Philippines. In Papua New Guinea, outside intervention led by New Zealand resulted in a truce between government forces and the separatist Bougainville Revolutionary Army. In the Philippines, government policies of national reconciliation have resulted in agreements over the past two years with the two main Muslim groups in the south and the establishment of an autonomous region. The threat from the New People's Army has been receding, but the government is also seeking negotiations on this front.

The Cambodian situation presented a sharp contrast. In early July, Second Prime Minister Hun Sen launched a military action against First Prime Minister Prince Norodom Ranariddh, claiming that the latter was colluding with the Khmer Rouge. Ranariddh's forces put up little resistance, except in defense of one small base along the Thai border. In contrast to the Cambodian conflict in the 1980s, the fighting in 1997 was limited and outside forces were not tempted to intervene by proxy. Ranariddh's considerable international support moved the struggle to the diplomatic arena with a focus on the July 1998 elections. These elections and the manner in which they are conducted will likely be a source of intense debate among the Cambodian parties and outsiders interested in Cambodia. The elections will legitimate the winner only if they are seen as being scrupulously fair.

In Indonesia, preelection tensions aggravated by the economic crisis combined to increase internal turmoil. Over the past two years, Indonesia has experienced numerous incidents. Many of these have had an anti-Chinese dimension, fanning this long-standing ethnic tension. Internal discontent seems likely to increase in 1998, making domestic stability in Indonesia one of the uncertain and risky elements in the Asia Pacific security outlook. So far, however, there is no institutionalized resistance to the central authorities.

NEW SECURITY ISSUES   Aside from the financial crisis, a number of other issues are increasingly cited by strategic specialists as nonconventional security issues. In responses to a questionnaire, they ranked the environment high among the "new" security issues. This was given added emphasis in 1997 because of the severe and prolonged haze over Singapore, Malaysia, and parts of other neighboring countries as a result of Indonesian forest fires. The haze is primarily regarded as a human security issue affecting personal health and well-being, but it also has the potential to become an international relations problem because of public dissatisfaction in affected countries over the lack of enforcement of regulations in Indonesia. The Association of Southeast Asian Nations (ASEAN) is seeking to develop a cooperative framework to handle the issue.

Drug smuggling is also seen as an acute and growing problem by many of the security analysts. Other new security issues cited by security specialists include transnational crime, smuggling, piracy, and illegal migration.

REGIONAL COOPERATION   Governments in the region continue to be supportive of regional cooperation, particularly ASEAN, ARF, and APEC. During 1997, ASEAN expanded its membership from seven to nine with the addition of Laos and Myanmar. The addition of the latter was a matter of some controversy as both the Europeans and North Americans let it be known that they preferred to work with an ASEAN that did not include the Myanmar regime.

Despite this official support, the regional cooperation movement in Asia Pacific may be losing some of its momentum as the initial enthusiasm for new schemes wears off. There is increased questioning of the payoff from all the time and money spent on meetings. APEC, which has agreed to bring its membership up to 21 with the admission of Peru, Russia, and Vietnam, as well as ASEAN wrestle with the greater complexities of achieving a work program with a more diversified membership. Moreover, the region's financial crisis overshadowed the trade- and investment-oriented agendas of ASEAN and APEC and called into question the usefulness of these institutions in dealing with the overriding financial concern.

For APEC and the more recently formed ARF, meeting expectations will become much tougher as these institutions move from an early stage of promise (vision) to a new phase of implementation (action). Many of the regional issues, whether achieving new rules of the game in trade or resolving the complex territorial issues of the South China Sea, are inherently difficult, and the creation of multilateral regional entities and dialogue in and of themselves only marginally contributes to their resolution. The growing recognition of this has helped spawn the upsurge in bilateral high-level diplomacy, both independently of and alongside the multilateral institutions, and new interest in small, flexible plurilateral groupings, of which the Four-Party Talks and KEDO are examples. The long-term development of a true Asia Pacific security community, in which there is no expectation of the use of coercion, will be built through many different fora and over a long period of time. The *Asia Pacific Security Outlook* in its own small way is one such endeavor.

ASIA PACIFIC SECURITY OUTLOOK 1998

1 Australia

THE SECURITY ENVIRONMENT

Like its Labor predecessor, Prime Minister John Howard's Liberal-National coalition government, which was elected in early 1996, sees the regional security environment as relatively benign. No threats to Australia are envisaged for the foreseeable future. But the coalition also sees the region's security future as uncertain. Optimists within government and the security bureaucracies tend to believe that the huge economic stake in regional stability shared by all East Asian states will, on balance, enhance regional security. Pessimists believe that changing power balances, unresolved sovereignty disputes, uneven economic development, and possible future conflicts over resources mean that the future is likely to be unstable and that widespread violent regional conflict cannot be ruled out. The rise of Chinese power is a source of particular concern, although this is rarely articulated publicly.

Initially there was little public comment by officials on the security implications of the current financial crisis in East Asia. General John Baker of the Australian Defense Force (ADF) maintained that Australia's strategic environment was "relatively benign." However, official analyses projected that the sharp downturn in regional economies might have worrying implications for domestic security, particularly in countries where grossly unequal disparities in wealth correlate with ethnic differences or the economic downturn is paralleled by drought-induced agricultural failure, as in Indonesia.

Australia reacted promptly to the currency crisis with multimillion dollar loans to Thailand and Indonesia. Australia's reaction may have been influenced by security considerations, but the driving motivation was economic. Australia sees its own future economic prosperity as tied inextricably to that of its East Asian neighbors. Thus the assistance was seen by the government as being in Australia's direct national economic interest.

While economic downturn has obvious potential security risks, it will also lead to a reduction in regional defense buildups. In this respect, it will reduce Australian concerns over a regional arms race or a rapid closure of the technological lead on which Australia's defense planning continues to depend.

Defense Policy and Issues

DEFENSE POLICY   Perhaps in response to the pessimistic view of regional security, the coalition government has proved more willing to embrace radical change in Australia's security policy than most analysts had expected. In April 1997, the Defense Efficiency Review spelled out sweeping changes in defense management practices which will eventually cut 7,800 defense jobs and place a further 13,000 at risk. Much of the projected A$1 billion (US$650 million at A$1 = US$0.65) in savings, about 10 percent of the defense budget, will be used to increase the ADF's combat capability, which currently only receives about 20 percent of budget resources.

The review, swiftly approved by the cabinet and currently being implemented, recommended an acceleration of the Labor-initiated program of privatizing nonvital defense functions and the introduction of modern business practices where appropriate to enhance efficiency. It also recommended the creation of a unified command structure. The three services will retain their separate identities, but their independence will be curtailed.

Major changes to the structure of the Australian army were announced in October 1996. Greater emphasis is to be placed on firepower, intelligence, and mobility. The army had been suffering from shortages of trained personnel and inadequate equipment; it lacked mobility and was unable to fight effectively at night. The reform program will require, among other things, a shift away from traditional protective missions and the acquisition of additional helicopters and light armored vehicles.

The increased emphasis on defense capability was reflected in the

Strategic Review completed in December 1997, an unclassified version of which was released publicly. The review stresses the need for the ADF to be more assertive in the face of potential military threats in the region and calls for an expansion in the ADF's strike force capability.

THE DEFENSE BUDGET   The coalition government plans to spend more on defense in real terms in the future. Notwithstanding budgetary cutbacks in many other portfolios, the defense budget remained untouched again in 1997. The estimated defense budget for fiscal year 1997–98 is A$10.4 billion (US$6.8 billion), approximately the amount China claims to spend on defense. This represents an increase of A$400 million (US$260 million) over fiscal 1996–97. However, the defense share of gross domestic product for fiscal 1997–98 is estimated to be 1.9 percent, the same proportion as fiscal 1996–97 and one of the lowest in Asia Pacific. Defense outlays are projected to be 8.2 percent of total fiscal 1997–98 outlays, compared with the estimate of 7.8 percent in fiscal 1996–97. Defense expenditure on capital projects for fiscal 1997–98 will be A$3 billion (US$2 billion).

A$2.3 billion (US$1.5 billion) will be spent in fiscal 1997–98 on already approved major capital equipment projects, including:
- ANZAC frigates—A$439 million (US$285 million)
- C-130J transport aircraft and logistic support—A$264 million (US$172 million)
- Collins Class Submarines—A$192 million (US$125 million)
- coastal mine hunters—A$179 million (US$116 million)
- upgrade of P3C surveillance aircraft—A$72 million (US$47 million)
- light armored vehicles—A$56 million (US$36 million)
- Jindalee Radar Network—A$34 million (US$22 million).

The government has approved new major capital equipment projects with a total cost of A$579 million (US$376 million), of which A$37 million (US$24 million) is to be spent in fiscal 1997–98. These projects include:
- upgrades to the navy frigates
- acquisition of seabed mines
- enhanced electronics for anti-ship missile decoy systems
- enhancement of army surveillance and reconnaissance assets
- improved communications for the ground force
- enhancement of the F-111 strike capability

- improved communications for air defense and electronics for the aircraft control system.

The government has also approved new major capital facilities projects with total project costs of A$176 million (US$114 million), of which A$45 million (US$29 million) is planned to be spent in fiscal 1997–98. A further A$419 million (US$272 million) in spending is planned for fiscal 1997–98 on other capital facilities.

The Department of Foreign Affairs and Trade (DFAT), whose security responsibilities include arms control, disarmament, and regional security dialogue, has undergone far fewer radical changes than the Department of Defense. However, in the government's cost-cutting drive DFAT's share of resources was reduced in both fiscal 1996–97 and fiscal 1997–98.

In mid-1997, DFAT published a white paper, the first produced by any Australian government. The report places great stress on Australia's vital economic relationships with the region but makes no radical departures from Labor policy. There are differences of emphasis, but many are rhetorical rather than substantive. One official described the white paper as an exercise in "product differentiation."

ALLIANCE RELATIONSHIPS   The promised "upgrading" of the alliance relationship with the United States took place in 1996. President Bill Clinton's visit to Australia at the end of the year was generally seen as a success for the coalition government. In a significant departure from Labor security policy, U.S. and Australian officials discussed combined U.S.-Australian "contingency response" operations in the region and "active support" by Australia for forward-deployed U.S. forces. Australia also strongly supported the enhancement of the U.S.-Japan security relationship embodied in the defense guidelines agreement signed between Washington and Tokyo in September 1997. These developments have led critics to claim that the Howard government is taking Australia back to a policy of "forward defense"— preparing once again to fight with allies far from Australian shores. Defense Minister Ian McLachlan dismisses all such claims, although he had previously suggested that Australia might send forces to fight in a war on the Korean peninsula. The term now used by the government to describe Australia's defense posture in the region is "forward cooperation."

Early in 1996, the government offered the United States the right to pre-position military supplies permanently in Australia's north.

Washington apparently was not interested. But at the 1996 Australia-United States Ministerial Consultations (AUSMIN), the two sides agreed to "set up a specific program of action to implement enhanced U.S. armed forces use of Australia's northern training ranges." There has been some speculation in Australia, denied by both U.S. and Australian officials, that training facilities in Australia might replace those in Okinawa.

The future of the once-controversial U.S.-Australian Joint Defense Facilities at Pine Gap and Nurrungar was raised at the AUSMIN talks. In the joint statement, the governments endorsed a 10-year extension of and expressed "their commitment to long-term continuation" of the Pine Gap arrangement. They also agreed to effect "new arrangements" following the planned closure of Nurrungar around the year 2000. Nurrungar's closing will mean that Australia's *active* role in the U.S. early-warning system will also cease. However, the Howard government remains committed to assisting U.S. missile defense efforts, and the communiqué noted that cooperation in "counter-proliferation," including "scientific collaboration on ballistic missile defenses" had been "intensified."

The October 1997 AUSMIN talks largely continued the themes from 1996. The joint statement predictably stressed the strength and vitality of the bilateral relationship. It noted that U.S. and Australian security are inextricably linked and that the alliance rests on the "twin pillars of flexible, highly capable, and interoperable defense forces and close bilateral consultations on security issues of mutual interest."

Contributions to Regional and Global Security

RELATIONS WITH EAST ASIA   In the run-up to the 1996 election, Labor had claimed that a coalition government would lack any real commitment to Asia and would have little credibility among Asian leaders. Despite some initial difficulties, there is little evidence to support such a claim today. Coalition ministers, like their Labor predecessors, stress that relations with Asia are Australia's "highest foreign policy priority." In the wake of the 1997 Southeast Asian currency crises, Canberra reemphasized its commitment to the region, reflecting Australia's vital economic and security interests in East Asia.

Australia's relations with regional states have been hurt, however, by the high media profile of Pauline Hanson, the one-time Liberal

Party candidate who is now an independent member of Parliament. Hanson's reactionary populism, in particular her opposition to Asian migration, has won considerable support in the Australian heartland where unemployment rates are high and the future appears uncertain. But it has also harmed Australia's image in the region and brought criticism of Howard for not doing enough to counter Hanson's extreme views.

MULTILATERAL AND BILATERAL APPROACHES   As expected, the Howard government has continued to pursue Labor's policy of multilateral security engagement with the region while also stressing what it calls "practical bilateralism." The latter has led to agreements to conduct bilateral security consultations with South Korea and Japan and to expand dialogue with China to include regional security issues.

Official rhetoric makes it appear that Indonesia has become a less important security partner for Australia than it was under the Labor government. But in practice little has changed. Australia now conducts more military exercises with Indonesia than it does with the United States.

Papua New Guinea's internal convulsions and the civil unrest in Bougainville are very much a security concern for Australia, but less as a direct threat than because of the long colonial and postcolonial relationship between the two countries. With the possibility of the collapse of government and major political unrest in Port Moresby following the Sandline affair (see the Papua New Guinea chapter), there was media speculation about possible Australian military intervention. But while the government prepared to send forces to help evacuate Australian citizens if necessary, there was never any real possibility of military intervention to restore order and manage an interim administration.

The bilateral relationship that caused the Howard government the most problems in 1996–97 was that with China. Beijing resented Australia's public support of the dispatch of U.S. carrier battle groups to the South China Sea during the Taiwan Strait crisis in early 1996 and made no secret of its displeasure at the "upgrading" of the U.S.-Australia defense relationship. Chinese concerns were increased by the AUSMIN reference to Australia and the U.S. Pacific Command sharing a "vision for combined operations" in the region and by the U.S.-Australian commitment to continuing cooperation in missile defense research. Relations between Beijing and Canberra were further strained by the high-profile visit of the Dalai Lama to Australia in September 1996, and by the visit to Taiwan by Australia's primary industry and energy minister in the same month. By late 1996, the atmosphere between the two countries had deteriorated to such an extent that ministerial visits were effectively banned by the Chinese.

Early in 1997, Canberra moved to reestablish better ties with Beijing. Visits by Australian ministers to Taiwan were banned and a request from Taiwan for two ministers to visit Australia was rejected. In a March 1997 fence-mending visit to Beijing, Howard told his hosts that Australia's foreign policy was based on a "clear-headed and *independent* assessment of the region." He insisted that the U.S.-Australia alliance was "not directed at anybody else."

The increasing importance of China as a trading partner was the primary motivation behind Canberra's efforts to rebuild the relationship with Beijing. A DFAT report published in April 1997 projects that China will become Australia's third largest trading partner by the end of the decade. Concern to preserve the relationship with Beijing determined Australia's decision to reject a U.S. request to cosponsor an anti-Chinese resolution at the UN Commission on Human Rights in April. Beijing commended Canberra's decision.

Coalition policy toward the rest of the region differs little from that of Labor. As with the Paul Keating government, the pursuit of Australia's economic interests is the primary driving force of the coalition's regional foreign policy. The exceptions (Myanmar, North Korea, Papua New Guinea, and other Southwest Pacific states), where political and strategic concerns override those of economics, were exceptions for Labor as well. The coalition government has also shared Labor's policy failures in the region. Neither has succeeded in persuading states like China, Indonesia, and Myanmar to embrace the sort of human rights regime that Australia believes is appropriate. The Howard team has been no more successful than Labor in persuading the United States to change agricultural export subsidy programs that harm Australia's farm exports, nor has the coalition done any better than Labor in gaining membership of the Asia-Europe Meeting despite support from Japan, Indonesia, and Thailand.

Foreign Minister Alexander Downer, who seems relatively less optimistic about multilateral approaches to security than his predecessor Gareth Evans, noted in 1996 that "it will take time to build trust and confidence between countries which have no tradition of discussing their security concerns and their approaches to national security." Nevertheless, the government continues strongly to support the ASEAN Regional Forum (ARF), for several reasons. First, multilateral forums like ARF can achieve things which are difficult to achieve in bilateral exchanges, notably the development of region-wide security-enhancing norms such as the peaceful settlement of disputes. Second, ARF provides valuable opportunities for ministers and senior officials to have discrete out-of-session bilateral meetings. Third, failure to participate in ARF would harm Australia's standing in the region.

ARMS CONTROL   On September 10, 1996, after years of discussion and two years of intense negotiation, the Comprehensive Test Ban Treaty (CTBT) was finally opened for signature at the United Nations. Securing a CTBT had long been a high-priority arms control goal for Canberra, and Australian diplomats played a critical role in securing the agreement after all efforts to achieve consensus within the Conference on Disarmament in Geneva had failed. DFAT successfully proposed seeking UN General Assembly adoption of the treaty, thus bypassing the impasse in Geneva.

The coalition was less enthusiastic in another area of arms control. Downer welcomed the report of the Canberra Commission on the Elimination of Nuclear Weapons but stopped short of endorsing the commission's argument that the abolition of nuclear weapons is both desirable and possible. The report was presented to the UN General Assembly in September 1996. While commending the report, Downer also noted that the commissioners "did not represent any government."

The government gave a cool reception to a mid-1996 International Court of Justice advisory opinion that the use or threatened use of nuclear weapons was generally contrary to international law. This view had been strongly supported by the previous Labor government, but Downer said only that the coalition government would "study it carefully." Canberra's primary concern, he said, was to ensure that current arms control efforts "are not undermined"—the clear implication being that the World Court ruling might have this effect.

PEACEKEEPING   Australia's commitment to peacekeeping has continued to decline under the new government. McLachlan attributes this both to the changing nature of peacekeeping and to the problems some UN member states have in paying for peacekeeping operations.

A further factor is the coalition's focus in its foreign and security policy more on Australian national interests than on "good international citizenship." While in 1993 Australia had some 1,000 troops engaged in peacekeeping operations in eight overseas locations, plus a further 1,100 committed to humanitarian relief in Somalia, by October 1996 only 65 Australian peacekeepers were deployed overseas, of whom only 32 were directly involved in "Blue Beret" UN peacekeeping operations.

2 Canada

The Security Environment

During 1997, the Canadian public's attention to Asia Pacific was captured by a series of high-profile events: the prime minister's "Team Canada" economic missions, the declaration of 1997 as the Canadian Year of the Asia Pacific, the transition of authority in Hong Kong, a scandal of a Canadian-based gold mining company in Indonesia, Canada's hosting of the Leaders' Meeting of the Asia-Pacific Economic Cooperation (APEC) forum in Vancouver, and the region's growing financial problems. Asian immigration to Canada remains at high levels (largely now from Taiwan and the People's Republic of China rather than Hong Kong), and disclosures about the illegal movement of peoples, drug trafficking, and transnational criminal elements with Asian connections have raised public awareness of (and thus government attention to) the need to address these human security and transnational problems both at home and in the region.

Continued economic growth in the region is regarded as critically important to Canada itself as well as to its objectives in Asia. As stated by one high-level Department of Foreign Affairs official, "Our economic priorities drive [Canada's] Asia Pacific agenda while our security objectives support and enhance them." Despite the recent turbulence in financial markets, Canadians continue to view Asia Pacific as a region of growth and opportunity, albeit a challenging place for Canadian entrepreneurs to penetrate. With the currency crises as only one sign of a more general uncertainty about the robustness and regularity of Asian financial markets, there is concern about the sustainability of economic growth and the consequences of an economic downturn or economic upheavals for the maintenance of domestic and regional stability. Trade with Asia dipped in 1996; the recent downturn in regional markets in 1997 will likely continue this trend.

Canadians believe that the opening of Asian societies and the emergence of consumer-oriented classes in them will almost certainly result in more participatory political systems and accountability by leaders, although not perhaps as rapidly or as "democratic" as Western publics may wish. But rapid socioeconomic change (upward, but especially downward) can create tensions and imperil regime and human security, as recent events in Indonesia show. Canada itself will suffer if political/economic systems are in turmoil, disrupting trade and investment, putting strains on bilateral and multilateral relations, and affecting the lives of the many Asian Canadians with family and business ties in Asia Pacific. Corrupt and irregular business practices, in which the state or state rulers are implicated, are increasingly raised by Canadian officials and private citizens as a problem in dealings with certain Asian states.

In political/security terms, the region is regarded as resting at a relatively peaceful geopolitical configuration. However, many Canadian defense analysts view this as a temporary condition. Uncertainties prevail throughout the region and dominate national security agendas and defense policies. From the geopolitical perspective, the rise of China, the decline of Russia, and the ambivalence of the United States regarding its regional role and commitments create fundamental uncertainties. In the short term, traditional territorial disputes (especially over maritime claims and resources) and nationalist impulses, coupled with the ideological stalemate on the Korean peninsula, highlight the risk of potential crises. Rising levels of defense spending and military hardware have been a cause for concern. Particularly troubling is the proliferation of missiles and missile technology and of nuclear-weapons-relevant technology and technicians in China, Russia, North Korea, Pakistan, and India.

The Canadian government views establishment of a multilateral regional framework for security as essential to ensure long-term regional stability. It places primary emphasis on its achievement through multilateral approaches of dialogue, cooperation, and institution building. During 1997, efforts to support regional groupings such as the Association of Southeast Asian Nations (ASEAN), the ASEAN Regional Forum (ARF), APEC, and associated track two ventures have continued. At the same time, a feeling has developed that the momentum in ASEAN and ARF may be stalled. Knowledgeable Canadians were apprehensive about the enlargement of ASEAN, in part because this signaled a form of "acceptance" of the Myanmar regime, and in part because adding two members with divergent economic and political systems would strain ASEAN decision-making norms of consensus and noninterference.

The internal turmoil in Cambodia, along with the news of domestic political/social tensions and humanitarian crises in other states, reinforced the Canadian perspective that internal dimensions of security are of crucial importance. A critical natural event or political/economic crisis could throw a major Asian state into chaos and with it the prospects for regional stability. Matters of human security, otherwise labeled as "unconventional" security threats, including issues of governance and the rule of law, communal conflict, sustainable development, and, closer to home, drug trafficking, money laundering, and illegal immigrants, have risen in importance on Canadian bilateral and multilateral agendas in the region. These are security concerns that are likely to remain continuing problems in coming years, leading the Canadian public to demand tighter regulation of immigration and more effective law enforcement and the Canadian government, whose unilateral capacity for effective action in these areas is limited, to seek increased bilateral and multilateral cooperation toward these ends.

Defense Policy and Issues

GENERAL DEVELOPMENTS   The Canadian Department of National Defense (DND) has continued to struggled with the implications of the end of the cold war for a defense establishment that had been largely oriented toward Euro-Atlantic priorities and commitments. The 1994 white paper set out the general parameters of Canadian security interests and defense policy, but it did not resolve the problems of a gap between commitments and capabilities, nor did it establish priorities for force reorganization and capital acquisition. A lack of continuity of military command and of political oversight has not helped in addressing these issues. In less than two years, the positions of chief of defense staff and minister of defense have each changed hands three times.

Over the last decade, the Canadian military structure, in terms of personnel and equipment, essentially has been determined by government budget-cutting priorities. A budget of Can$10.7 billion (US$7.4 billion at Can$1 = US$0.69) in fiscal year 1994–95 has declined to only Can$8.5 billion (US$5.9 billion) for fiscal 1998–99. Personnel levels will have dropped: there are now roughly 60,000 in uniform compared with 83,000 in the mid-1980s. During the last two years, critical decisions on equipment acquisition have been avoided, including the acquisition of new submarines and new naval helicopters. With the Canadian federal budget about to yield a surplus in fiscal 1997–98, the DND is optimistic that its financial situation will stabilize.

ASIAN DEFENSE ISSUES   Canadian Asia Pacific security interests are to promote a stable regional security framework, strengthen bilateral relations with key Asian states, limit weapons proliferation, and advance confidence-building, peacekeeping, and peace-building mechanisms. Ottawa's goal is to be a "useful and interesting participant" in Asia Pacific security affairs. To that end, the DND has taken steps to bring greater "balance" to its regional profile and distribution of resources. A Pacific affairs unit was created last year in Department Headquarters. The deployment of naval assets to Maritime Command Pacific helps meet the white paper commitment to achieve an Atlantic/Pacific balance.

The Canadian military has been drawn into increasing contact and interaction with Asia Pacific militaries in multilateral government and nongovernmental contexts. These involve regular exercises with other navies, as in the biannual RIMPAC exercises in the North Pacific and the MARCOT '97 exercises off the Canadian west coast, and active participation in seminars of military and security personnel.

Canada is making a particular effort to expand bilateral military relationships in Asia. The regularized program of ship visits by the Canadian navy, alternating between Northeast Asia (WESTPLOY '96 and '98) and Southeast Asia (WESTPLOY '97), has been important. These visits have raised Canada's profile in the region and provided Ottawa with opportunities for bilateral meetings with high-level military and defense figures in the region.

The Foreign Affairs and National Defense departments appear now to be in accord regarding military-to-military contacts as a mode of engagement with countries whose security policies and practices are of concern to Canada. This has been a particularly troubling issue vis-à-vis China and the People's Liberation Army, with military-to-military visits and meetings having been curtailed or canceled. However, policy has changed recently, with defense officials visiting each other's capitals and with the visit of a Canadian ship to China planned as part of WESTPLOY '98.

Contributions to Regional and Global Security

Canada maintains its long-standing security priorities, namely to promote effective global and regional institutions for collective security (especially the United Nations, the North Atlantic Treaty Organization, and the Organization for Security and Cooperation in Europe), to stem the proliferation of weapons of mass destruction as well as conventional weaponry, and to promote peace building, peacekeeping, and preventative diplomacy as modes of conflict management. The United Nations remains the focal point for Canada's peace and security initiatives. Canadian efforts within the UN context for 1997 focused upon advancing constructive reforms of the UN's finances and bureaucracy, reforming Security Council membership (including lobbying for a nonpermanent seat for Canada during 1998–99), and enhancing the UN's capacity to respond to complex humanitarian emergencies and conflicts through peacekeeping and peace building. Canada continued its strong support and active participation in UN (and other multilateral) peacekeeping missions.

The most prominent Canadian security-related initiative of 1997 was the government's support for the global campaign to ban land mines. Working in partnership with other governments and activist nongovernmental organizations (NGOs), this campaign proved remarkably successful. In December 1997, over 100 states gathered in Ottawa to sign a convention banning the production and deployment of land mines. In the coming year, advancing the ratification of the land mines convention and coordinating assistance to land mine victims will remain a priority of the government. The government will likely broaden its nonproliferation agenda to include other forms of conventional weaponry, and will continue its long-standing efforts to promote arms trade registers and transparency in both conventional and nonconventional weapons matters. It must be noted that Asia Pacific presents significant challenges in this regard. For instance, of the major powers in the region, only Japan signed the land mines convention.

Peacekeeping retains its traditional high priority for the Canadian government. Although the overall number of military peacekeepers has dropped substantially during the last year, the number of missions in which Canada has been involved has not; nor has the Canadian desire to take a leading role in the creation of missions or the enhancement of UN capacity to respond to complex humanitarian emergencies dampened. For example, Prime Minister Jean Chrétien mobilized a short-lived Canadian effort to spearhead a UN peacekeeping response to the crisis in the former Zaire. Post–cold war experience, however, has led to substantial evolution in the way Canadian policymakers regard "peacekeeping" and "peacekeepers." These are now seen as a component within peace building—a complex undertaking involving weapons clearance and control (including mines), humanitarian assistance, NGO activity in (re)constructing civil society, training civilian police, organizing and monitoring elections and courts, and other aspects. Given this complexity, the military has to plan and share organization and delivery responsibilities and train and assign personnel to undertake a host of nonmilitary activities.

Ottawa is convinced that furtherance of multilateralism and multilateral dialogue and institution building in Asia Pacific is essential to sustaining a meaningful Canadian role in regional security matters and to creating a regional system able to manage future security challenges. At official levels, Canada continues its active encouragement of the development of ARF. While somewhat restive with ARF's reluctance to deal with difficult issues, Canada concentrated its efforts on making progress on practical security questions in the ARF intersessional meetings. Peacekeeping and maritime cooperation have been the foci of these activities in the last couple of years.

Canadians also actively participate in the nonofficial regional track two dialogues that have proliferated dramatically throughout the 1990s. Canada seeks to solidify the organizational structure and substantive agenda of the Council for Security Cooperation in Asia Pacific (CSCAP). In this context, CSCAP's North Pacific Working Group is seen as particularly important. As the only mechanism that brings all the relevant players to the table, this working group not only sustains prospects for dialogue in this critical subregion but also maintains a role for Canada in the North Pacific context.

Two other long-standing Canadian track two programs in the

region continued in 1997, both funded through the Canadian International Development Agency (CIDA). These are the series of workshops and consultations among claimants in the South China Sea organized jointly with Indonesian partners and under the principal sponsorship of the ASEAN Institutes for Strategic and International Studies Asia Pacific Roundtable meetings, now in their 11th year.

While multilateral approaches are a hallmark of Canadian engagement in Asia Pacific, in recent years Ottawa has given renewed attention to key bilateral relationships in the region. There are various rationales for this. In part, it is the natural accompaniment to the current government's campaign of high-profile bilateral trade missions to Asian states. In part, it reflects Ottawa's appreciation of the realities of the region, especially Northeast Asia, where states regard their bilateral relationships as the foundation for developing or sustaining multilateral activity. In the last year, particular emphasis appears to have been given to advancing relations with China, Indonesia, and Japan, while sustaining the existing active relationship with South Korea. A jointly sponsored Canadian-Japanese track two experts' report on mutual interests in security cooperation was commissioned during the year, followed by the inauguration of bilateral politico-military talks. Official bilateral contact on security issues was expanded with China as well, with the first visits of high-level military and defense officials, and with increased Chinese involvement in Canadian track two seminars on arms control and multilateralism. The Canadian Member Committee of CSCAP also engaged in a series of bilateral consultations with its counterparts in Indonesia, Mongolia, and South Korea.

HUMAN SECURITY AND GOVERNANCE   The Canadian government is committed to basing its security policies on a broad definition of security, as encompassed in the phrase "shared human security," and to advancing the principles and practices of human rights, good governance, and the rule of law. Translating these statements of principle into foreign policies has proved controversial and challenging, both domestically and externally.

There is ample scope for use of a broad definition of security in Asia. The Canadian government, NGOs, and academics have advocated action be taken to mitigate a range of human security problems within and across Asian borders, including working conditions (especially for children); discrimination and violence against women; the illegal movement of peoples (especially women and children in the sex trade); the despoiling of forests, water, and air; and the employment of unsustainable agricultural practices. Canadian Foreign Minister Lloyd Axworthy has given considerable public visibility to these issues, advancing a broad vision for addressing the underlying social, economic, and environmental causes of human conflict and suffering. Peace building and societal reconstruction are areas to which Axworthy has channeled considerable bureaucratic and fiscal resources.

It is largely through CIDA that human security and sustainable development priorities are translated into programs in Asian countries. CIDA programs in Asia have increasingly targeted sustainable development, resource conservation, conditions of women and children, and grass-roots community building, moving away from funding traditionally conceived, large-scale infrastructure projects. In recent years, CIDA has quietly expanded its purview to support research on the causes and conditions of threats to human security. Such efforts included the establishment in 1997 of projects on "development and security in Southeast Asia" and on institution building in Vietnam.

Canadian media coverage, and thus public attention, has focused on "human rights." Fueled by a vigilant and vociferous NGO community, Ottawa has been castigated for being preoccupied with business and economic priorities, at the expense of "people priorities." Thus, the Chrétien government has tried to maneuver within the dilemma created by the apparent contradictions among its foreign policy goals. The outcome has been policies of "constructive engagement," entailing the symbolic raising of human rights issues by Canadian officials in bilateral and multilateral meetings with relevant Asian states, e.g., within ARF concerning Myanmar. The government has become convinced, however, that the most effective results are achieved by programs to advance the rule of law and instill "good governance." There has been a burgeoning of bilateral programs with Asian states in such areas as training police and judges, drafting legislation, and promoting civilian control of the military.

The role of NGOs in monitoring social conditions and in the delivery of humanitarian assistance and development aid has been deliberately enhanced by the Canadian government. NGOs are on the scene before and during the development of crises, and they remain after diplomatic and peacekeeping missions have left. Canada provides substantial resources to support NGOs and their activities in

Asia, including resources to facilitate participation by Canadian and Asian NGOs in large regional and international conferences such as the UN Women's Conference in China. The People's APEC Summits (coincident with the APEC Leaders' Meetings), with their various components on women, militarization, and the impact of globalization, have been supported by Canada in the Philippines in 1996 and Vancouver in 1997.

3 China

THE SECURITY ENVIRONMENT

The past year was unusually significant for China. The death of Deng Xiaoping, the Hong Kong handover, the 15th Party Congress, and President Jiang Zemin's state visit to the United States all had important direct or indirect implications for China's security outlook. The latter three developments occurred smoothly, much to the credit of Jiang. China also avoided the currency and financial crises affecting much of the rest of Asia.

POLITICAL DEVELOPMENTS   Coming only once every five years and establishing authoritative policy guidelines for the future, the Party Congress was the most significant political event of the year. Meeting in September, the 15th Party Congress determined the leadership of the Central Committee and filled posts in the Politburo and the Standing Committee. Major changes were made in the Central Committee, from which many older members were retiring. In Jiang's words, the infusion of many younger bureaucrats into the new Central Committee "proves that the party has marched a step forward in making the central collective leadership more revolutionized, younger, better educated, and more professional." The need for fundamental shifts in economic structure and growth was a central theme as the Party Congress called for an acceleration of the economic modernization and reform program by selling, merging, or closing many of China's state-owned enterprises. Jiang established an ambitious economic goal of doubling gross national product by 2010.

The Party Congress formally completed the power transition from the Deng Xiaoping era to the post-Deng leadership. This was a smooth transition without political unrest. While the Party Congress changed some of the personnel of the central leadership in China, it did not change the style and framework of leadership. China continues to have "collective" leadership at the central level, and this leadership appears to be stable and powerful.

Thus the economic reform program begun by Deng continues in the post-Deng era. This means that China will continue to emphasize the need for a stable security environment to facilitate its economic programs. Aside from this security implication of the 15th Party Congress, the Congress provided guidelines for continuing the effort to reduce military manpower while strengthening national defense through a better trained and equipped military.

As in many countries in the post–cold war era, social stability remains a major internal security issue in China. Because of the fundamental changes in the economy and society, the country is naturally facing new social challenges, such as equality, social mobilization, urbanization, population growth, unemployment, crime, and balance among the provinces. Among these issues, the more urgent problems involve social stability in the urban centers most affected by the restructuring and downsizing of state enterprises and in the areas dominated by minority populations.

In his report to the National People's Congress meeting in March 1997, Premier Li Peng acknowledged that crime and personal safety remain serious challenges. He also urged China to oppose words or actions that would damage national unity. In his report to the September Party Congress, Jiang pointed out that the reform process does create lawlessness; reaffirmed the importance of public security for personal safety, development, reform, and stability; and stated his determination that China must crack down on all kinds of crime. As part of its effort to meet the challenges of economic and social changes, China is doubling its endeavors to establish a social safety net through a workable social security system.

THE EXTERNAL ENVIRONMENT   Externally, China's security environment was perceived to be positively affected by the April 1997 five-party Agreement on Arms Reductions in Border Areas covering China's northern and western borders. This was offset, however, by the negative implications of the strengthening of the U.S.-Japan military alliance.

The Agreement on Arms Reductions in Border Areas. The Agreement on Arms Reductions, to be valid until 2020 and subject to renewal, was concluded among China, Russia, Kyrgyzstan, Kazakhstan, and Tajikistan and is the most significant event in Chinese and regional security during the year. The agreement requires the five countries to reduce military forces in the border areas to "a lower degree," appropriate to the prevailing friendship among the countries and having only defensive capabilities. The five countries agreed not to use or threaten to use force against each other, that none of them would seek military superiority over the others, and that the military forces in the region would not conduct offensive actions.

The agreement established a 100-kilometer-wide zone on each side of the border. In this region, the number of personnel and armaments are limited, with ceilings on each side of 3,900 tanks, 4,500 other armored vehicles, and 130,100 personnel. There should be a 15 percent reduction in troops over two years. The five countries also agree to exchange data on their military forces in the border area.

The agreement represents the culmination of arms reduction talks that began between China and the Soviet Union in November 1989 and expanded to five countries following the breakup of the USSR. In April 1996, the five countries had reached the "Shanghai agreement" on strengthening confidence building in military fields in the border area.

From the Chinese perspective, the Shanghai agreement and the 1997 arms reduction agreement have tremendous significance because they represent the success of a decade-long effort to normalize relations on the 7,000-kilometer border with the former Soviet Union, build confidence, and reduce military deployments. The Soviet Union had been China's biggest strategic threat for three decades from the early 1960s through the late 1980s, and these agreements symbolize the end of the Soviet/Russian threat.

The U.S.-Japan Security Alliance. The Chinese regard the strengthening of the military alliance between Japan and the United States, especially the new Guidelines for U.S.-Japan Defense Cooperation, as the most negative development for China security over the past two years. Chinese leaders and analysts have articulated four major concerns:

- The strengthening of the military alliance runs contrary to the general regional trend of promoting peace and security through increased political and economic ties and dialogues.

- The scope and function of the U.S.-Japan alliance has shifted from protecting Japan to assuming responsibility for the whole Asia Pacific region.
- The guidelines now give Japan a regional security role in the "surrounding area," including the entire Asia Pacific region.
- The bilateral security arrangement encompasses Taiwan, a part of China, and this is totally unacceptable to China.

The Chinese reject U.S. and Japanese arguments that because the alliance has served to protect regional stability and prosperity, China also has been a beneficiary. Contrary to the view that the alliance protected stability, the period since the alliance was created in 1960 has witnessed the Vietnam War, conflict in Cambodia, high tensions in the Korean peninsula, and other signs of instability. Nor has the alliance been a cause of prosperity, which must be largely attributable to the economic policies of the individual countries of the region.

Chinese also reject the argument that the defense guidelines are not geographic in nature. U.S. officials maintain a "strategy of ambiguity" that avoids stating clearly whether the scope of the U.S.-Japan Security Treaty covers Taiwan. However, they affirm that the treaty is intended to deal with regional uncertainties, and when they discuss regional uncertainties they always mention three areas: the Korean peninsula, the Taiwan Strait, and the South China Sea. Two of these three refer directly to China, making it obvious to Chinese that China is a principal target of the treaty.

Japanese officials have been clearer than the Americans on the Taiwan question. The former chief cabinet secretary, the deputy foreign minister, the assistant to the prime minister, and others have all stated that the treaty does cover Taiwan. They say that this is not new because the area of the Far East included Taiwan since the treaty was first adopted in 1960. However, at that time both Japan and the United States had diplomatic relations with Taiwan rather than with the People's Republic of China. Now that the two countries' relations with the People's Republic are normalized, a continued commitment to the defense of Taiwan is regarded in Beijing as contrary to the declared one-China policy of Japan and the United States.

Sino-American Relations. China's relationship with the United States is not necessarily a direct security issue at the present time. However, relations with the United States affect China's security, economic development, political stability, and national unity. For the Chinese, national security has become more and more an issue of political and economic relations with others. The year 1997 marked the first time since 1989 that there was no major crisis in relations with the United States, despite China's unhappiness with the U.S.-Japan defense guidelines. Jiang's visit to the United States changed not only the environment but the direction of Sino-American relations. During the visit, for the first time, the two sides articulated a goal of their post–cold war relationship as achieving a "constructive strategic partnership." This helped reduce Chinese suspicions of the U.S. strategic intention toward China and in East Asia, and should provide opportunities for positive developments in relations between mainland China and Taiwan as well as for strengthened bilateral and multilateral cooperation between China and the United States.

Other Issues. The Four-Party Talks involving North and South Korea provide a good example of cooperation between China and the United States on regional security issues. Three rounds of preparatory talks were held in 1997 as well as the first formal meeting in Geneva in December. The Chinese government believes that a peaceful mechanism can be established for the peninsula through dialogues between the two Korean governments and the Four-Party Talks. There is basic optimism in China about future developments in the Korean peninsula following the South Korean election in December 1997.

Internal developments in Cambodia were a matter of concern. The Chinese government, however, no longer supports any one faction in Cambodia. It is hoped that peace, stability, and economic progress in that country can be restored and sustained for the good of the region as well as the people of that country.

Relations with the member countries of the Association of Southeast Asian Nations (ASEAN) improved during 1997, a year in which almost all major Chinese leaders visited the area. One important positive development was the mitigation of tensions over territorial disputes in the South China Sea. During his visit to Malaysia and Singapore, Li stated that if the territorial disputes cannot be resolved by this generation, China would like to leave them for future generations to resolve. A joint statement between China and the ASEAN countries in December reinforced their determination to refrain from individual action before reaching a final solution to the disputes.

China enhanced its energy security through two major oil agreements with Kazakhstan, concluded during Li's one-day visit to that country in September. Economic cooperation will promote better relations between the two countries and assist them in maintaining stability in the border area. The leadership in Kazakhstan reassured the Chinese side that they would not allow activities in Kazakhstan designed to encourage separatism in China.

Defense Policy and Issues

BASIC DEFENSE POLICY   The 15th Party Congress set the basic direction for defense policy for the coming five years. Two particular results are important.

First, the Congress reaffirmed the current national security strategy:
- China should press ahead with modernization and reform in order to make the People's Liberation Army (PLA) a more revolutionary, up-to-date, and standardized force.
- China will adhere to the strategy of active defense, based on fewer but better troops.
- In order to adapt to the profound changes in the global military arena, the defense forces should intensify training and education, and upgrade capabilities with modern technology.
- More efforts should be given to defense-related science and technology. Defense industries should adapt to the needs of the socialist market economy, improving their productivity and management.
- The people's awareness of the importance of national defense should be strengthened through public education.
- The militia and reserves should also be strengthened as well as the Chinese People's Armed Police and the public and state security departments.

Second, Jiang announced that following the reduction of armed force personnel by one million in the 1980s, China would further reduce personnel by 500,000 in the four-year period from 1997 to 2000, from nearly three million today to 2.5 million at the turn of the millennium.

These two decisions effectively continue the strategy of "Qualitative Army against Limited and High-Tech Warfare," adopted by Deng and other party and military leaders since the late 1980s. The importance of this shift was underscored by the Gulf War, which gave the Chinese a vivid picture of modern warfare. Previously, China's main defense objective was to counter a large-scale invasion involving ground warfare. Its current objective is to handle a limited, local war fought with high-tech weapons in the land or sea border areas of China. This scenario requires fewer military personnel with more advanced weaponry.

THE NEW SECURITY CONCEPT   Another important development in China's post–cold war security strategy is the introduction of the "New Security Concept." This concept was first officially elaborated at the ASEAN Regional Forum (ARF) meeting in Beijing on confidence-building measures in March 1997 and in April was incorporated into the Sino-Russian Joint Statement on the Multilateral World and Establishing a New International Order. The joint statement, signed by Russian President Boris Yeltsin and visiting Jiang, argued for an end to "cold war thinking," as represented in efforts to strengthen military blocs, and argued that states should resolve issues peacefully "through dialogue and consultation, seeking peace and security through bilateral and multilateral coordination and cooperation." The Agreement on Arms Reductions was held up as an example of a new security model.

In a speech to the fourth ARF meeting in Malaysia on July 28, 1997, Foreign Minister Qian Qichen further elaborated that in the new international situation, "security cannot depend on increasing military weapons, nor can it be dependent on military blocs. Security should depend on mutual trust and the linkage of common interest." He outlined four dimensions of enhancing regional security: equal, friendly, and stable relations among states; economic development, exchange, and cooperation; peaceful means of resolving disputes; and dialogue and cooperation. In Qian's view, as an experiment in regional security cooperation, ARF itself represents the New Security Concept.

BUDGET ISSUES   The state budget allocated 80.57 billion yuan (US$9.7 billion at renminbi 1 = US$0.12) to defense in fiscal year 1997, according to the budgetary report to the People's Congress in March. This represented 12.7 percent growth over the previous year's defense spending, equaling the overall growth in the state budget in fiscal 1997. This rate surpasses the 8.1 percent inflation rate in 1996, but it is lower than the growth rate on state enterprises (19.1 percent), agriculture (13.8 percent), education (13.8 percent), or science (13.8 percent). In his report to the People's Congress, Li called for strengthening defense science research, technological development, and equipment development and production.

According to General Cao Gangchuan, chairman of the State Commission for Science, Technology, and Industry for National Defense, civilian production now accounts for 80 percent of defense industry production. China's policy for weapons development calls for "more research than production." At the PLA's plenary meeting on equipment, General Zhang Wannian, vice chairman of the Central Military Commission, called for more selectivity in military equipment development, focusing on fewer key areas.

General Wang Ke, head of the PLA's Logistic Department, has indicated that military production and businesses are major sources of income to make up for shortages in the defense budget.

Contributions to Regional and Global Security

China continued to strengthen its contribution to regional and global security in 1997. At the regional level, the significance of the Agreement on Arms Reductions has already been discussed. This agreement is regarded not only as being significant for China's security and for regional stability in itself but also as a precedent for other agreements.

China's other regional efforts included:
- Food aid to North Korea, with 150,000 tons committed during the first half of the year. China is participating in the Four-Party Talks to replace the 1953 armistice and strengthen peace and stability on the Korean peninsula.
- Visits by naval ships to Malaysia, the Philippines, Thailand, the United States, and other Asia Pacific nations to promote mutual understanding.
- Intensified participation in the intergovernmental ARF dialogue process by co-hosting a meeting on confidence-building measures in Beijing in March. At the track two level, a Chinese national committee for Asia Pacific security cooperation was organized and joined the Council for Security Cooperation in Asia Pacific in 1997. China also participated in the track two Northeast Asia Cooperation Dialogue.
- More bilateral security dialogues with other countries in the Asia Pacific region. China and Japan held two rounds of security consultations in March and December. The 10th meeting of Chinese and Australian security and disarmament consultations took place in December, and China and the United States held the first

meeting of deputy-minister-level security talks, a mechanism for regional security dialogue between high-level defense and military officials established by Jiang and U.S. President Bill Clinton in Washington in October.
- Continued talks with Vietnam and India on border issues.

At the global level, China has continued to make progress on arms control. In early August, the Chinese government issued regulations on nuclear material and technology exports that establish a stricter export control system for nuclear material, equipment, and technology. On September 16, China formally joined the Zanggar Committee, the international group that coordinates nuclear supplier efforts to control nuclear exports. On October 22, the Chinese government issued regulations on the export of military goods, intended to strengthen coordination and control over such exports.

In early May, China decided to join the standby arrangement for UN peacekeeping, thus committing itself to providing military observers, civilian police, and other supporting personnel for UN peacekeeping operations.

4 The European Union

The Security Environment

The security involvement of the European Union in Asia Pacific is peripheral and, given the political nature of the EU, complex. Apart from geography, EU involvement is peripheral because European security policies (which for the most part are conducted in and through the North Atlantic Treaty Organization [NATO]) are focused on the Euro-Atlantic region and its surrounding areas. European involvement in Asia Pacific security is small, both by the standards of Asia Pacific security requirements and as a share of overall European resources committed to security.

Europe nevertheless clearly has important security interests and objectives in the region, and increasingly it has become aware of them. Economic involvement in Asia Pacific is substantial. At US$388 billion in 1995, Europe's trade with Pacific (East and Southeast) Asia accounts for about 25 percent of extra-EU trade and is equivalent to about three-quarters of U.S. trade with the region. Europe's direct investment stakes in Pacific Asia are also important. During the 1990s, European annual foreign direct investment flows to Pacific Asia roughly equaled those from the United States. European banks have extended significant amounts of credits to the region. In short, European stakes in the stability and prosperity of Asia Pacific are almost as weighty as those of the United States. Unlike the United States, however, Europe does not (and could not) try to protect its interests through a large military presence. Rather, it has to rely on others, primarily the United States. European countries individually and jointly do, however, maintain resources and commitments in Asia Pacific that cumulatively are quite substantial.

European involvement in Asia Pacific is also complex. As a political entity, Europe continues to be both more and less than the sum of European countries: more, because the EU has developed some capacity to design and implement common foreign policies, and European relations with Asia have been one of the areas where common policies were developed. Less, because the degree of policy cooperation and coordination among EU member states remains limited, and member countries continue to pursue different, and sometimes even rival, policies in Asia.

Since the early 1970s, there has been an institutionalized dialogue between the EU and the Association of Southeast Asian Nations (ASEAN). In March 1996, 25 heads of state and governments and the president of the European Commission, in a summit meeting in Bangkok, launched the Asia-Europe Meeting (ASEM) process, in which the EU explores a broad agenda of economic, cultural, political, and security issues of common concern with (presently) 10 countries from Pacific Asia (the ASEAN-7* plus China, Japan, and South Korea). During 1997, ASEM developed considerable momentum, with a flurry of meetings both at the level of senior officials (including ministers of economics and finance, as well as the political directors of the foreign and trade ministries) and among representatives of business, track two, and nongovernmental organizations. The consecutive meetings of EU-ASEAN and ASEM foreign ministers in Singapore in February 1997 were perhaps the most significant among the meetings of 1996–97. After that, the issue of Myanmar's involvement in those multilateral activities grew serious between ASEAN and the EU, resulting in the cancellation of an important gathering between the two groups in late 1997.

The capacity of the EU to conduct a common foreign and security policy edged forward as a result of the Amsterdam summit meeting of the EU in June 1997. Among the useful if modest developments were the designation of a senior European official in charge of coordinating the work of the Council of Ministers (the EU's key decision-making forum) as the representative voice of European foreign policy, the formation of a policy planning and analysis unit in Brussels, and the

* ASEAN-7 refers to Brunei, Indonesia, Malaysia, the Philippines, Singapore, Thailand, and Vietnam.

decision to enable the EU to develop "common strategies" (i.e., broad policy guidelines as well as specific policies). But decisions on any common strategy or policy will still require consensus, and the limitations of the EU in developing common approaches to international issues was strikingly illustrated by a falling-out of member countries at the UN Commission on Human Rights in Geneva in April 1997, where a draft resolution on China cosponsored by the United States and Denmark failed to secure the support of several key EU member states.

Those events underlined once more that member governments, not the EU, continue—even after Maastricht and Amsterdam—to be the primary locus of European foreign policy making. Parallel to multilateral dialogues, therefore, European countries also have been enhancing bilateral relations with Asia. France continued its new Asia policy with visits by President Jacques Chirac to China (announcing a "strategic partnership") in May 1997 and to Southeast Asia in November. But the formation of a Socialist-led government under Lionel Jospin significantly weakened the president's grip on foreign policy. The new Socialist-led government has yet to show a commitment to Chirac's Asia policies. In the United Kingdom, too, the new Labour government sent mixed signals about its willingness to continue the Asia policies of its Conservative predecessor. Foreign Secretary Robin Cook did visit Southeast Asia in September 1997, but he also made public his support for excluding new ASEAN member Myanmar from the London ASEM meeting (which had been tacitly dropped, anyway) and declared the government's intention to develop more restrictive, human-rights-oriented policies on arms sales. In Germany, a revolt by parliament against the government's policy toward the Tibet issue in mid-1996 jolted relations with China; it took several months and considerable efforts by the Bonn government to bring the relationship back on an even keel. Italy moved to close the gap between its political relations with Asia and those of the three other major European countries with the region through visits by Prime Minister Romano Prodi in East and Southeast Asia in late 1997.

Overall, European involvement in Asia Pacific over the last year has been marked by two somewhat contradictory trends. On the one hand, Pacific Asia's economic development attracted European countries' efforts to strengthen their presence in, and their ties with, the region. When the financial market turbulence hit the region, some of those efforts were revealed to have been imprudent; thus European banks had increased their exposure to the region in the course of the year before the crisis broke more than had American banks, and by late 1997 they carried more high-risk debts. The turmoil in the second half of the year clearly heightened European awareness of and interest in the region and added a new dimension to the growing understanding of Europe's very substantial stakes in Pacific Asia.

On the other hand, European governments found it difficult to sustain their determination to strengthen relations with Asia, as several major projects—the European Monetary Union and the enlargement of EU and NATO—gathered momentum and absorbed political energies. The financial and economic upheavals in Pacific Asia were generally assumed to have no major implications for Europe, and there was thus no sense that Europe should or could contribute to managing the crisis, other than by backing initiatives by the United States and the International Monetary Fund (IMF). Domestic social and economic problems and the changes in governments in France and Britain did not help, either. As a result, efforts to strengthen Euro-Asian relations were mostly taken up by the EU in multilateral fora, while bilateral policy efforts took the back seat.

Defense Policies and Issues

The principal trends in European defense policies—continued substantial real cutbacks in defense expenditure, enhanced emphasis on multilateral military operations, and the restructuring of armed forces away from conscript armies toward military professionalism, enhanced technological prowess, and versatility—have no direct relevance to security in Asia Pacific: they are geared toward the new security environment in and around Europe after the end of the cold war. However, the new emphasis on mobility and multinational forces will also tend to enhance European capabilities for operations outside Europe.

Defense expenditures in three of the four major Western European countries—France, Germany, and Italy—continued their downturn in 1996 and 1997. Only in the United Kingdom was a rise in real defense spending projected for 1997. Total spending of all European NATO members also declined substantially in real terms, from US$158 billion in 1996 to US$144 billion in 1997 (measured in 1996 dollars). This represented about 2.2 percent of gross domestic product (as compared with 3.1 percent in 1985). During this decade, the combined manpower of European NATO forces had shrunk by about a quarter, from 3.14 million to 2.44 million. Procurement, however, has begun to grow again in real terms, underlining the efforts to restructure European armed forces in line with changing requirements.

In Asia Pacific, Europe's principal direct military presence during 1997 further declined as a result of the Hong Kong handover, which involved the withdrawal of Britain's limited military presence there (the 1,400 strong Ghurka infantry brigade was transferred to Brunei). Britain continues to participate in the Five Power Defense Arrangements (FPDA), however, and in fact intensified its involvement in the FPDA through large-scale participation in joint exercises in 1997. France maintained its military presence involving some 8,000 soldiers and the Pacific Naval Squadron with three frigates, some patrol vessels, reconnaissance aircraft, and patrol ships in the South Pacific. A reflection of France's position in the South Pacific is the permanent presence of a French liaison officer at the headquarters of the U.S. Pacific Command in Hawaii.

France's military presence in the region expresses its considerable strategic interest in Asia Pacific, as its three possessions form one of the largest single maritime claims to exclusive economic exploitation of ocean resources. Yet its possessions also constitute a liability: they depend on substantial financial support from the motherland, while portraying France as a colonial power. Serious social tensions and political discontent with French rule in the possessions add to this image. France's nuclear test sites in the region have been dismantled, and France has indicated its willingness to sign and ratify the Treaty on the Southeast Asia Nuclear-Weapons-Free Zone, subject to the resolution of some open issues.

Apart from those remnants of a direct military involvement in Asia Pacific, European countries have recently strengthened other, more temporary forms of presence. These include flag-showing and joint exercise visits, such as the U.K. Ocean Wave '97 naval and air deployments or the 1997 visit of a German naval unit to Japan.

Contributions to Regional and Global Security

Europe's arms sales to the region are one of the most important European contributions to security in Asia Pacific. Whether this contribution is positive or negative is a matter of controversy, depending upon one's viewpoint and the specific circumstances. After the end of the cold war, the share of European arms sales to Pacific Asia has tended to edge up; it now corresponds to about 20 percent of total Pacific Asian arms purchases. International Institute for Strategic Studies data show that from 1992 to 1994 Western European suppliers accounted for some 35 percent of ASEAN's total arms purchases, and close to 60 percent of South Korea's. The largest individual defense contracts are those between France and Taiwan for 16 frigates of the La Fayette class and 60 Mirage 2000 fighter aircraft, of which Taiwan in 1997 started to take delivery. Under pressure from China, Paris has rescinded further contracts with Taiwan.

Largely in the context of arms sales, a number of European countries also have reached bilateral defense-cooperation agreements with Pacific Asian countries. The United Kingdom has such agreements with most ASEAN countries (Brunei, Indonesia, Malaysia, the Philippines, Singapore, and Thailand) as well as with several other states in the region. Agreements covering procurement (Brunei), joint exercises and training (Singapore), and logistics (Australia) were signed in 1997. France has similar agreements with five ASEAN countries (of which those with Singapore and Vietnam were signed in 1997) and South Korea, as have Sweden (with Singapore and Malaysia) and the Netherlands (South Korea). France, Germany, and the United Kingdom also maintain bilateral security dialogues with Japan involving the ministries of foreign affairs and defense, and France has a similar dialogue with China.

Visits and exercises, both individually and jointly, of European naval and air forces in the region are another contribution to regional security. Although they must be seen largely in the context of European arms sales, they also provide useful contributions to mutual understanding, to habits of cooperation, and to levels of training. During 1996 and 1997, the United Kingdom conducted 16 joint and eight national military exercises in the region. France also regularly exercises with other countries in the region, as it did with Singapore in 1997.

Apart from bilateral security consultations, Europe also participates in a number of multilateral security dialogues in Asia Pacific. They include the ASEAN Regional Forum (ARF), the Council for Security Cooperation in Asia Pacific (CSCAP), and the FPDA (in which the United Kingdom is the only European member). European involvement in ARF is somewhat awkwardly organized through participation of the country currently holding the rotating six-month presidency of the EU, plus a European Commission official as notetaker. This led France and the United Kingdom to submit formal bids for separate participation in ARF in 1996, a matter still pending. Europe participates vigorously in track two security dialogue processes, notably—but not only—through the European chapter of CSCAP.

Europe's contribution to the security of Asia Pacific is perhaps most important in the context of a broadly defined "comprehensive" understanding of the term. Thus, the EU is among the major donors of official development assistance to Pacific Asia's developing economies, and several European countries (among them Belgium, France, Germany, Italy, the Netherlands, and the United Kingdom) provided financial support for the December 1997 IMF emergency package to South Korea. The EU has assumed membership in the Korean Peninsula Energy Development Organization with an important financial contribution of US$86 million, and several European countries have made additional individual contributions. The EU also provided the most generous response (US$69 million) to the UN appeal for food aid to North Korea. This aid was explicitly justified not only on humanitarian grounds but also as a European contribution to preventing destabilization of the region.

Comprehensive security also plays an important role in multilateral dialogues between the EU and Pacific Asia, namely in the context of EU-ASEAN and ASEM. The EU-ASEAN and ASEM agendas include discussion of issues related to regional and global security, such as the situations on the Korean peninsula, in the Middle East, and on the Balkans, as well as freedom of navigation, efforts to curb weapons of mass destruction, and the so-called new security agenda of terrorism, drugs, and environmental degradation. Such issues are also taken up in bilateral security consultations between EU member states and Pacific Asian countries.

European involvement in Asia Pacific security continues to evolve, reflecting a growing awareness of Asia Pacific's importance to Europe (and vice versa). In this, Europe has clearly benefited from the region's shift toward multilateralism, as Europe's limited national resources, as well as its own policy traditions, heavily favor multilateral involvement. There is nevertheless still a considerable lack of cohesion to European approaches to Asia Pacific, and the sum total of its influence remains less than it could be.

Even if European countries were able to pool their resources more effectively, however, European involvement in Asia Pacific security would continue to be supportive, rather than independent. Today, Europe's modest but substantial involvement in regional security seems more relevant than it is often given credit for. This is particularly true if security is understood in a broad sense. Here, European contributions have helped significantly to underpin a benign and reasonably stable regional order.

5 Indonesia

The Security Environment

INTERNATIONAL AND REGIONAL SECURITY   Indonesian security analysts believe that the end of the cold war has eliminated the prospect of a world war at least for the foreseeable future. Increasing interdependence among Asia Pacific countries also has improved the security outlook in the region. The whole Western Pacific has become one interdependent region in economic, political, and even security terms. Beyond that, a common political consciousness is developing, in which all the parties feel they are in similar situations and face similar challenges.

Nevertheless, numerous local and regional conflicts persist. Indonesia's immediate surrounding area is no exception. For example, Indonesia and Malaysia have a territorial dispute over the Sipadan and Ligitan islands off the coast of Kalimantan that has been exacerbated in recent years because of national sensitivities and the resource potential of the area. However, in an effort to resolve the issue amicably, Indonesia accepted Malaysia's suggestion that the matter be put to the International Court of Justice.

The Indonesian Department of Defense and Security issued its second white paper in 1997, assessing the changing strategic environment in the East Asian region and updating the earlier version prepared in 1995. With Russia effectively out of the regional equation, the white paper is based on the view that the triangular relationship between China, Japan, and the United States is the key to regional strategic stability for the foreseeable future. The white paper endorses the new Guidelines for U.S.-Japan Defense Cooperation. This reflects the Indonesian government's judgment that the U.S.-Japan alliance, along with Japan's lack of nuclear weapons or significant power projection capability, plus the countervailing power of China, make a Japanese threat to the region unlikely. Rather, China is seen as the main potential threat to the region and Indonesia's sovereignty. Continued successful economic growth will increase China's power, while failure could lead to a flood of refugees into Southeast Asia. Finally, the white paper foresees more room for the Association of Southeast Asian Nations (ASEAN) to play the role of a major pole of power in the new regional environment.

The white paper also makes reference to nontraditional security issues in the region. These include fish poaching, safety of navigation (as in the Strait of Malacca), and energy resources. And in the latter months of 1997, Indonesia had direct experience with two other nontraditional issues: the environment and economic crises. The drought-fueled forest fires in Sumatra and Indonesian Kalimantan in September and October greatly disrupted normal life and caused serious danger to the health of citizens in neighboring Malaysia, the Philippines, and Singapore. This led to an unprecedented apology by President Suharto to the governments of the other countries affected, as well as to the beginnings of coordinated action by all the affected states to attempt to meet the crisis and reduce the chances of repetition in the future. The regional economic crisis triggered by the Thai currency devaluation in July had a progressively more serious impact on Indonesia's economy through the end of the year. In early September, the government announced the first of several austerity packages to meet the crisis and bolster the country's currency and financial markets. In October, it made an agreement with the International Monetary Fund (IMF) for funding and reforms. For the Indonesian people, the crisis underlined the economic interdependence and vulnerability of the increasingly globalized economy.

DOMESTIC SECURITY CONCERNS   Despite the problems, the Indonesian government views the external security setting as generally benign at present. By contrast, internal security is a subject of continuing and increasing concern for Indonesia's leadership.

Prior to the 1997 economic crisis, Indonesia's success in economic development had been widely acclaimed. This success was measured in terms of economic growth rates, the development of physical infrastructure, the achievement of near self-sufficiency in food, and declining rates of population growth and absolute poverty. However, it is widely perceived that rapid economic growth has been accompanied by a growing gap in standards of living between the rich and the poor. This gap is most conspicuous in the urban centers. As a result of the economic crisis, employment levels and earnings have been reduced, the removal of subsidies on basic commodities required by the IMF will raise prices, and the ranks of the poor and desperate are again increasing. The resulting rise in social tensions and volatility, further compounded by political uncertainty over the succession to Suharto, is a serious issue.

Another issue with consequences for domestic security is the challenge of economic globalization. Concerns about globalization among the political and military elite have been reinforced by the 1997 economic crisis. While recognizing that it is impossible for Indonesia to isolate itself from globalization and that it brings some positive benefits for the development process, government leaders worry that the negative aspects of globalization may hamper development. Some in the military see globalization as an attempt by developed countries to dominate the whole world through science and technology. There is also concern among government leaders that globalization may threaten social and cultural values.

An even more fundamental challenge for Indonesia is to maintain national unity within a highly diverse society. While progress has been achieved in building a sense of national unity across cultural and linguistic lines, largely through improved communication and the spread of the national language, ethnic and religious divisions remain sharp. The years 1996 and 1997 saw a series of violent clashes between ethnic and religious groups virtually across the archipelago, evoking memories of bitter and bloody internal conflicts in the first two decades of Indonesian independence.

Defense Policy and Issues

DOCTRINE   At the level of basic doctrine there has been little substantive change in recent years. Indonesian defense policy remains based on the concept of total defense. The geopolitical concept of *Wawasan Nusantara* (Archipelago Concept) codifies and reflects the

Indonesian government's commitment to maintaining the territorial integrity of the 17,508-island archipelago and control over the resources within its jurisdiction.

At the more operational level, however, changes are under way. The Indonesian navy and air force are at the forefront of the process. In November 1997, for example, the Indonesian navy launched a reconsideration of the long-excluded possibility that the navy could play a role in military operations other than war. Indonesia's air force is conducting a similar assessment.

There are several reasons behind this reconsideration. Both the navy and the air force were generally unhappy about the military's Dual Function (or *Dwifungsi*) concept. This doctrine legitimizes a broad civil and political as well as security role for the military, but in practice it had been used to support a political role for the army, to the exclusion of the other services. The rethinking of operational doctrine has also stemmed from the impact of modern technology on military affairs.

PROCUREMENT How these changes will eventually be reflected in defense procurement is difficult to project. Indonesia's defense budget (US$2.3 billion at late-1997 exchange rates) is approximately 1.3 percent of the country's gross domestic product, the smallest percentage among the countries of Southeast Asia. Yet the ratio between routine expenditure (personnel, operations, and maintenance) and developmental expenditure (infrastructure and equipment) is nearly 3 to 1. Indeed, more than a quarter of the defense budget is allocated to the police force. These factors mean that in practice defense procurement is affected more by budgetary limits than doctrinal or operational requirements.

The role and management of Indonesia's defense industry continued to be a controversial issue in 1997. In recognition of the limited purchasing power of the Indonesian Armed Forces (ABRI), the government's Strategic Industry Management Agency, run by Minister of State for Research and Technology B. J. Habibie, has set a target of 20 percent of its total output to be dedicated to defense production. This target has yet to be met. For its part, ABRI has long been dissatisfied with the cost competitiveness and appropriateness of some of the items supplied by the strategic industries. ABRI's dissatisfaction is magnified by the lack of reliable information on the strategic industries' accounts. For these and other reasons, in 1997 presidential backing for Habibie and his various projects seemed to be waning. For example, supervision of the purchase of Russian Sukhoi fighter aircraft was assigned to Minister of State for National Development Planning Ginandjar Kartasasmita instead of Habibie. As of the end of 1997, the competition among various interests in the government over the role and control of defense production and procurement was unresolved.

The 1997 financial crisis will further constrain military procurement (as well as government support for the domestic defense industry) for the foreseeable future.

DEFENSE COOPERATION Indonesia has long-standing security cooperation and contact with regional countries and the United States as well as Australia. Within ASEAN, especially with Malaysia and Singapore, Indonesia has conducted joint exercises involving all three of the services. Military exchanges with other Southeast Asian countries, such as the Philippines, are of lesser priority and are focused more on resolving common security concerns than on defense cooperation in the narrow sense. The objectives of defense cooperation with the United States and Australia are to assist in the development of Indonesia's defense capability and to bolster general regional security, since both countries can potentially be called upon for regional defense.

Indonesian-U.S. cooperation experienced a setback in 1997. The U.S. emphasis on human rights issues and other elements of democratization once again affected Indonesian-U.S. relations, including defense cooperation. Reacting to rising criticism of Indonesia, especially from the U.S. Congress, Suharto in June canceled a planned purchase of U.S.-made F-16 fighter aircraft and announced that Indonesia would no longer participate in the U.S. military training program (IMET). However, these steps did not result in major breaks in Indonesian-U.S. military relations, nor were they particularly costly to Indonesia's defense capability. Indonesian defense planners knew that, at a time when the global arms market is becoming much more pluralistic and competitive, it would not be difficult to find other suppliers of new aircraft. As for training, Indonesian leaders appear to believe that training in the United States will be resumed in time, probably with a different name but similar substance.

Defense cooperation with Australia has significantly improved. The Indonesia-Australia Security Agreement of December 1995 enhanced the two countries' already established military cooperation. What role this arrangement will play in the future in dealing with regional security problems is not clear. But the timing of the agreement, shortly after the seizure by China of Mischief Reef in the South China Sea (which was also claimed by the Philippines) at least suggested that the agreement could have greater significance and utility than just as an effort to enhance bilateral security relations.

There had been some criticism within Indonesia of the Indonesia-Australia Security Agreement. However, this criticism has been mostly based on doctrinal considerations (perceived contradictions with Indonesia's national resilience and nonaligned policies) rather than from the strategic point of view. ABRI leaders have long recognized that Australia is actually an appropriate source of military training because the two countries' forces are more comparable in size and resources than the Indonesian and U.S. militaries.

Contributions to Regional and Global Security

The Indonesian military and security policy leadership believes that Indonesia's primary contribution to regional security is through its participation and leading role in ASEAN. Indonesia believes strongly that regional cooperation can serve as a cushion to dampen conflicts or differences in the relations of the nations involved, and that the "ASEAN way" has been an effective and culturally appropriate means of fostering this cooperation. Furthermore, by serving as a stabilizing force in Southeast Asia, ASEAN directly contributes to maintaining broader regional stability. In addition, the ASEAN grouping gives its members collective influence and leverage in wider regional councils and even to an extent on the global level as well (such as through the ASEAN-Europe series of meetings).

These considerations underlie Indonesia's strong support for ASEAN continuing in the role of host and guiding force in the ASEAN Regional Forum (ARF) security dialogue process. Indonesia takes this position despite ARF's broad membership, which includes Northeast Asian states as well as the Americas, and the desire of some of the other members to change the name and operating procedures to an Asian Regional Forum.

Similar reasoning is the basis for Indonesia's active sponsorship and support of the widening of ASEAN to include all 10 states located within the geographic area traditionally identified as Southeast Asia. Thus Indonesia supported the admission of Myanmar (along with Laos) to ASEAN in 1997, despite the problems of Myanmar's human rights record and the potential complications in ASEAN dealings with the United States and Europe due to widespread international disapproval of Myanmar's military regime. Indonesian officials have argued that to leave Myanmar isolated from the regional grouping would only invite efforts by non–Southeast Asian powers such as China to establish a special relationship with the Myanmar regime and use this position as a basis for expanded influence in the region. Although the admission of Cambodia, which would complete the ASEAN-10, was postponed due to the mid-1997 coup by the Hun Sen faction and resulting questions about the legitimacy and efficacy of the post-coup government, Indonesia also favors the admission of Cambodia as soon as the status of its government is resolved.

While Indonesia supports military cooperation such as joint exercises with its immediate neighbors and other ASEAN members, it has continued to be more cautious about multilateral or ASEAN-wide cooperative security activities. Similarly, it has not supported the expansion of the ARF agenda or mandate to include practical security cooperation—although some ABRI leaders are reported to favor an evolution of ARF in this direction.

More broadly, Indonesia continues to support the concept of confidence-building measures, including greater transparency in the security area through such instruments as the UN Register of Conventional Arms. While recognizing that such measures are neither unqualified nor in themselves a panacea, the Indonesian government views them as a generally useful means of reducing fears of aggressive arms acquisition or intent and helping to promote security and stability.

Indonesia has been a contributor to international peacekeeping operations under the United Nations starting as early as the UN Congo operation in the early 1960s and continuing through the major Cambodian operation in the early 1990s. In 1997, Indonesian personnel were involved in UN operations in Bosnia. Indonesia is not a major troop contributor to these UN missions, due to budgetary and other constraints. But it continues to support the concept of a leading UN role in dampening and helping resolve international conflicts.

6 Japan

The Security Environment

Japanese view the emerging security environment in the Asia Pacific region with mixed feelings. The Russian military threat to Japan declined with the ending of the cold war, and the continuing U.S. commitment to regional and Japan's security are welcome; yet the potential for instability and conflict in the region raises significant security concerns for Japan.

Polls show the majority of the Japanese believe that the Japan-U.S. alliance is essential for the peace and stability of the Asia Pacific region. The revised Guidelines for U.S.-Japan Defense Cooperation, issued in September 1997, provide for a continuing U.S. presence in the region by revitalizing mechanisms for defense cooperation between Tokyo and Washington not only in the case of threats or attacks against Japan but also in the case of regional contingencies. Concerns have, however, been raised about the concentration of U.S. bases on Okinawa and social problems such as aircraft noise and crimes in areas surrounding U.S. bases, as well as about some aspects of the new guidelines (as discussed below). The persistent and growing trade surplus that Japan has with the United States remains a source of friction.

Japanese are deeply concerned about the prospect of great instability on the Korean peninsula, which would be a potentially serious threat to Japanese security. In particular, Tokyo is apprehensive of Pyongyang's intentions and its military capabilities, including its potential to develop nuclear, biological, and chemical weapons of mass destruction and the long-range missiles to deliver them. This apprehension continues despite Japanese support for North Korea's nuclear energy development through the Korean Peninsula Energy Development Organization (KEDO); the nascent thaw in relations between Japan and North Korea, exemplified by Pyongyang's allowing Japanese wives of North Koreans to return to Japan for temporary visits; and Japan's food aid. Other thorny issues between Tokyo and Pyongyang include the suspected abductions of Japanese nationals and North Korea's demand for compensation for the damage and suffering incurred during the 36 years of Japanese colonial rule in Korea and during World War II. With South Korea, Japan has a friendly but delicate relationship. The unresolved territorial dispute over Takeshima Island (Tok Do Island to the South Koreans) remains a source of tension between the two countries.

Japanese are also watchful of political and economic developments in China and that country's military activities in the region. China's nuclear capability, its substantial increase in defense expenditure, along with its claims to the Senkaku Islands (called the Diaoyu Islands by the Chinese) in Okinawa Prefecture, cause Tokyo considerable concern. Japanese believe that a politically stable China is essential to regional security, and that China's constructive cooperation and participation in regional economic and political dialogues are critically important for the stability and prosperity of the Asia Pacific region.

Russia's uncertain future, the unresolved Northern Territories issue, and Russia's deployment of offensive military capability in the Far East are other sources of concern. In particular, Tokyo's continuing preoccupation with the territorial issue has long limited its foreign policy options vis-à-vis Russia. Yet there are signs of change in Japan's foreign policy toward Russia and, for that matter, the Eurasian continent. In July 1997, Prime Minister Hashimoto Ryutaro launched a new "Eurasian diplomacy" intended to strengthen Japan's central Asian role. The November 1997 summit meeting between Hashimoto and Russian President Boris Yeltsin marked a major breakthrough in relations between the two countries. Both leaders agreed to do "the utmost" to conclude a peace treaty by the year 2000, based on the October 1993 Tokyo Declaration. Japan's strong support for Russian membership of the Asia-Pacific Economic Cooperation (APEC) forum signified the long-awaited rapprochement between the two countries.

Japan has a long-standing interest in promoting stability and development in Southeast Asia, and in protecting its access to sea lines of communications in that region. Tokyo considers multilateral fora such as the ASEAN Post-Ministerial Conferences and the ASEAN

Regional Forum (ARF) to be important mechanisms for security policy consultations with the Southeast Asian countries. Japan's bid for a larger political role, exemplified in Hashimoto's January 1997 speech in Singapore, met with cautious reservations from the member countries of the Association of Southeast Asian Nations (ASEAN). However, Hashimoto's July 1997 decision to deploy Air Self-Defense Force C-130s to Thailand to prepare for a possible evacuation of Japanese nationals from Cambodia met with little opposition abroad, despite domestic opposition.

The financial and currency turmoil in Asia was of increasing concern during the second half of the year, especially in November and December when the turmoil spread to Northeast Asia. Japanese became apprehensive about social stability in the region and the economic impact on Japan itself, whose capital-strapped banks are the primary foreign lenders in the developing Asian economies. The crisis heightened Tokyo's awareness of the degree of interdependence in the world economy and the potential not only for gains but also for great vulnerabilities.

Other security issues that concerned Japanese include transnational problems such as environmental degradation and terrorism. Even after a series of international and domestic crises such as the 1991 Persian Gulf War, the Great Hanshin-Awaji Earthquake in Kobe in 1995, and the Aum Shinrikyo sarin gas attacks on Tokyo subways in 1995, Japan remains ill-prepared to respond to crises. This was underscored again in the January 1997 oil spill in the Sea of Japan from the wrecked Russian tanker and by Tokyo's helplessness during the four-month (December 1996 to April 1997) seizure of hostages at the Japanese ambassador's residence in Lima.

On the domestic front, there has been a growing consensus in Japan that fundamental change is needed. Administrative reform and deregulation were pushed in the context of one of the severest economic recessions in the post–World War II Japanese economy and at a time when Japan's unwieldy bureaucracy had become the focal point of criticism for policy failures and coverups. The Asian financial crisis caused stronger outside pressure on Japan to stimulate its own economy to help absorb more Asian imports. With delicate support from the Social Democratic Party and the New Party Sakigake, the Liberal Democratic Party (LDP) government has been promoting reforms in six major areas: the structure of government, the economic structure, financial markets, the fiscal system, the social security system, and the education system. In December 1997, the cabinet endorsed the government's Administrative Reform Committee report calling for a reduction in the number of central government bodies from the current 22 ministries and agencies to 13, including the Prime Minister's Office, by 2001. Along with streamlining the bureaucracy and strengthening the prime minister's leadership role in strategic decision-making on diverse policy issues, a key objective of administrative reform will be to strengthen the functions of the cabinet so that Japan's political leadership will be able to respond effectively to emergencies. But the idea of upgrading the Defense Agency to a ministry, strongly proposed by the LDP's three defense-related committees, was withdrawn from the administrative reform agenda. Also, the cabinet announced in mid-December a plan to establish a special fund to help bail out the troubled financial system and a surprise ¥2 trillion (US$15.4 billion at US$1 = ¥130) income tax cut.

Defense Policies and Issues

DEFENSE OBJECTIVES   Two fundamentals of Japan's postwar defense policies are Article 9 of the Constitution renouncing the use or threat to use force and the Japan-U.S. alliance providing the ultimate security guarantee. Japan's white paper on defense, which has been published annually since 1976, describes the main features of Japan's defense policies that flow from these fundamentals. The first is its "exclusively defense-oriented policy," meaning that military force cannot be exercised until Japan is attacked, and that Japan's defense capability must be limited to the minimum necessary level for self-defense. The second is Japan's pledge that it will never become a military power that might pose a threat to other countries. The third consists of the three non-nuclear principles of not possessing, producing, or permitting the introduction into Japan of nuclear weapons. The fourth is Japan's commitment to civilian control of the military. Consistent with these basic policies and constraints, the Japanese government has been endeavoring to build an effective defense capability and strengthen the Japan-U.S. security arrangements.

In November 1995, the Japanese government adopted the new National Defense Program Outline (NDPO). The new NDPO, unlike the 1976 NDPO, specifies new roles and missions for the Self-Defense Forces (SDF), including response to large-scale disasters, terrorist attacks, and "various other situations that could seriously affect Japan's peace and security," and participation in UN peacekeeping operations. Based on the new NDPO, the Mid-Term Defense Program (MTDP) was adopted in December 1995. The MTDP provides the details of defense buildup in a specified period of time from fiscal year 1996 to fiscal year 2000. The ceiling of total defense-related expenditures required for the plan's implementation was estimated at approximately ¥25.15 trillion (US$193 billion) at fiscal 1995 prices. In 1997, however, as part of fiscal austerity measures, the government decided to review the program.

Under the MTDP, reorganization of major units and other organs has been carried out. In January 1997, the Defense Intelligence Headquarters was established under the Joint Staff Council to enhance intelligence collection and analysis capabilities.

DEFENSE SPENDING AND PERSONNEL The Japanese defense budget for fiscal 1997 was ¥4.9 trillion (US$38 billion), a 2.1 percent increase over the previous year. The ratio of defense spending to gross national product was projected to be 0.959 percent in 1997. This defense budget included ¥6.1 billion (US$47 million) earmarked for relocating some of the U.S. military facilities on Okinawa, as approved by the Japan-U.S. Special Action Committee on Okinawa (SACO). About 43.0 percent of the fiscal 1997 budget will have been spent on personnel and provisions, and 16.3 percent on front-line equipment. In June 1997, in view of the tightening fiscal situation, the government decided to curb increases in defense spending over the next three years, starting with fiscal 1998. The total expenditure of ¥25.15 trillion (US$193 billion) set forth in the fiscal 1996–2000 MTDP is to be cut by ¥920 billion (US$7 billion)in fiscal 1998–2000.

Japan's defense-related expenditure includes the costs of the SDF, research and development, the maintenance of the living environment around defense facilities, host-nation support for the U.S. forces in Japan, and the management of the Security Council. The budget does not include spending on the coast guard or pensions. Host-nation support came to ¥273.7 billion (US$2.1 billion) in 1997. It is expected that the fiscal 1998 defense budget will fall in real terms for the first time in the history of the SDF.

The SDF comprises the Ground Self-Defense Force (GSDF) with 150,070 members, the Maritime Self-Defense Force (MSDF) with 43,311 members, and the Air Self-Defense Force (ASDF) with 44,975 members (as of October 1996). It has about 47,400 reserves. The new NDPO envisages 160,000 troops for the GSDF, of which 145,000 members will be regular personnel and 15,000 will be Ready Reserve Personnel.

PROCUREMENT   Japan's current procurement aims to achieve the force levels set forth in the new NDPO (see table 1). Emphasis is placed on rationalization, effectiveness, compactness, and the qualitative improvement of defense capability.

Major equipment that Japan procured or started to procure in fiscal 1997 includes the following: The GSDF, 18 Type-90 tanks, three armored vehicles, 10 artillery, nine multiple launch rocket systems (MLRS), one antitank helicopter (AH-1S), four multipurpose helicopters (UH-60), two transport helicopters (CH-47), three OH-1 helicopters, and four surface-to-surface missiles (SSM-1); the MSDF, two 4,400-ton-class destroyers, one 2,700-ton-class submarine, one 510-ton-class minesweeper, one 2,400-ton-class training support ship, seven patrol helicopters (SH-60J), one rescue flying boat (US-1A), and two rescue helicopters (UH-60J); and the ASDF, eight fighter-supports (F-2), three rescue helicopters (UH-60J), four rescue and search aircraft (U-125A), and 13 intermediate-level jet trainers (T-4).

Japan procures most of its equipment from domestic sources or licensed production. Its ban on arms exports limits the growth potential of its defense industry, which accounts for only about 0.6 percent of the total value of Japan's domestic industrial production.

THE NEW GUIDELINES FOR U.S.-JAPAN DEFENSE COOPERATION
In September 1997, the governments of Japan and the United States issued the new Guidelines for U.S.-Japan Defense Cooperation. The geopolitical imperative underlying the revision of the guidelines is the potential for instability and conflict in the Asia Pacific region. The Gulf War and the more recent North Korean nuclear crisis in the spring of 1994 sensitized both Tokyo and Washington to the weaknesses in the framework for defense cooperation between the two countries in times of crisis. In April 1996, Hashimoto and U.S. President Bill Clinton reaffirmed the importance of the Japan-U.S. alliance as a stabilizing factor in the Asia Pacific region and agreed to review the 1978 guidelines. To achieve a degree of transparency in formulating the new guidelines, the two governments released a "Progress Report" in September 1996 and an "Interim Report" in June 1997.

Table 1. National Defense Program Outline in and after Fiscal Year 1996 (annexed table)

GSDF	Self-defense personnel	160,000
	Regular personnel	145,000
	Ready Reserve Personnel	15,000
	Major units	
	Regionally deployed units	8 divisions
		6 brigades
	Mobile operation units	1 armored division
		1 airborne brigade
		1 helicopter brigade
	Ground-to-air missile units	8 antiaircraft artillery groups
	Main equipment	
	Battle tanks	Approx. 900
	Artillery	Approx. 900
MSDF	Major units	
	Destroyer units (for mobile operations)	4 flotillas
	Destroyer units (regional district units)	7 divisions
	Submarine units	6 divisions
	Minesweeping units	1 flotilla
	Land-based patrol aircraft units	13 squadrons
	Main equipment	
	Destroyers	Approx. 50
	Submarines	16
	Combat aircraft	Approx. 170
ASDF	Major units	
	Aircraft control and warning units	8 groups
		20 squadrons
		1 squadron (airborne early warning squadron)
	Interceptor units	9 squadrons
	Support fighter units	3 squadrons
	Air reconnaissance units	1 squadron
	Air transport units	3 squadrons
	Ground-to-air missile units	6 groups
	Main equipment	
	Combat aircraft	Approx. 400
	Fighters (included in combat aircraft)	Approx. 300

SOURCE: Defense Agency, *Defense of Japan 1996*, p. 284.

The new guidelines provide a comprehensive framework for defense policy consultation and coordination between Tokyo and Washington both in peacetime and during contingencies. The core remains the same: in the case of an armed attack against Japan, the SDF will conduct defensive operations and the United States will take care of offensive measures.

Nonetheless, the new guidelines differ in some important respects.

First, they emphasize the need for active peacetime security cooperation to stabilize an international security environment by promoting regional security dialogues, participating in UN peacekeeping operations, and conducting emergency relief operations. Second, the new guidelines incorporate the concept of joint Japan-U.S. operations of their respective ground, maritime, and air forces when conducting bilateral operations in the case of an armed attack against Japan. Third, the scope of Japan's noncombat support operations in the case of regional contingencies has been clarified and expanded to include logistic support for U.S. combat forces, enhanced surveillance operations, minesweeping, interception of contraband on the high seas, measures to deal with refugees, and noncombatant evacuation procedures. Fourth, the new guidelines envisage the creation of two institutions, "a comprehensive mechanism" for joint defense planning and the establishment of common standards and procedures, and "a bilateral coordination mechanism" for specific activities in times of crisis. These mechanisms will involve all the relevant agencies of the two countries so that new laws or revised laws necessary for the implementation of the guidelines may be formulated and enacted.

If implemented smoothly and effectively, the new guidelines may mark a watershed in the history of the Japan-U.S. alliance. However, difficult problems remain. First, Japan's domestic laws and regulations need to be reviewed, and new laws enacted or the existing laws revised to make alliance arrangements envisaged in the guidelines viable. The 1996 Acquisition and Cross-Servicing Agreement regarding Japan's peacetime assistance for U.S. forces also needs to cover emergencies. Moreover, because of the political sensitivity and intra-bureaucratic conflict these issues involve, strong political leadership and public support will be required to implement the guidelines. Second, some of the operations envisioned for regional contingencies are politically controversial. Critics argue that Japanese minesweeping in international waters or rear area support for U.S. forces' activities can be seen as exercising the constitutionally forbidden use of force for collective defense. Third, there is no timetable for the implementation of the new guidelines, and because the guidelines "will not obligate either government to take legislative, budgetary, or administrative measures," implementation may stretch out indefinitely. Yet to delay the implementation too long risks undermining the alliance, as the United States will be uncertain of Japanese support in times of crisis. Fourth, the new guidelines define "areas surrounding Japan" as a "situational" rather than "geographical" concept, yet some critics argue the new guidelines tacitly cover the Taiwan Strait, creating tension in Sino-Japanese relations.

The new guidelines have important implications for Japan's security posture and for the Asia Pacific region. A continuing U.S. presence in Asia Pacific is assured by the new guidelines, and Japan's security role has been expanded in some respects, including noncombat support operations in regional contingencies. The implementation of the new guidelines will require Japan to upgrade specific capabilities of the SDF, such as airlift and sealift capabilities and intelligence-gathering capabilities.

While many countries in the region, including South Korea, welcomed the new guidelines, China expressed strong objections about the enhanced scope of the Japan-U.S. alliance in responding to regional contingencies, which could include a crisis in the Taiwan Strait. China's explicit objection to the guidelines triggered new interest in triangular security dialogues among Japan, the United States, and China to avoid misunderstandings or tension.

U.S. BASES   Okinawa Prefecture, accounting for only 0.6 percent of Japan's total land area, provides for 75 percent of U.S. bases in the country. Local resentments in Okinawa over the heavy concentration of U.S. bases and crimes, especially the September 1995 rape of a schoolgirl by U.S. Marines, awoke much sympathy in the wider Japanese public. In these circumstances, the Hashimoto government has sought to reduce and consolidate U.S. bases in Okinawa, while maintaining the capabilities and readiness of U.S. forces in Japan. In November 1995, Tokyo and Washington established SACO to make recommendations along these lines. The committee's April 1996 interim report announced the relocation of the U.S. Marine Corps' Futenma Air Station, which is in a densely populated area of Okinawa, within five to seven years. The final report, released in December 1996, called for the return of 11 U.S. military facilities, accounting for approximately 21 percent of the total acreage of the U.S. bases in Okinawa. However, the return of seven of these are contingent on successful relocation within the prefecture. To relocate Futenma, the two governments planned to build an offshore heliport facility off Nago. But a victory by opponents of the project in a December 1997 nonbinding vote in Nago raised questions about the political viability of relocation plans within Okinawa and thus of the SACO recommendations.

Contributions to Regional and Global Security

THE JAPAN-U.S. ALLIANCE   Given the great uncertainty and complexity of the post–cold war Asia Pacific region, the Japan-U.S. alliance remains a key to the stability and prosperity of the region and hence an important stabilizing factor in the international order. The strengthened Japan-U.S. alliance not only ensures the U.S. commitment to regional security but also constitutes the foundation for Japan's broader contributions to international security, encompassing many issues such as arms control and disarmament, the prevention of the proliferation of weapons of mass destruction, the North Korean nuclear issue, the Middle East peace process, and the peace implementation process in the former Yugoslavia, as set out in the U.S.-Japan Joint Declaration on Security issued at the April 1996 Hashimoto-Clinton summit.

SUPPORT FOR REGIONAL AND GLOBAL INSTITUTIONS   Although the Japan-U.S. alliance remains the linchpin of Japan's foreign and security policies, the Japanese government has been making substantial contributions to strengthening a variety of multilateral institutions.

In the economic field, Japan has been playing an active part in APEC since its inception in 1989. To increase economic ties between Asia and Europe, Japan hosted the first economic ministers conference of the Asia-Europe Meeting in September 1997. In the security field, Japan is keen to strengthen multilateral frameworks such as ARF for regional security policy consultation. Tokyo also has been playing a part in the nascent regional mechanisms for track two diplomacy, such as the Council for Security Cooperation in Asia Pacific and the Northeast Asia Cooperation Dialogue.

Japan's pursuit of a plutonium-based nuclear fuel cycle has generated an interest in regional nuclear energy cooperation at both the bilateral and multilateral levels. Reflecting proliferation concerns, various proposals for an ASIATOM or PACATOM (modeled on the European Atomic Energy Community, or EURATOM) have been put forth by former officials and academics.

At the global level, the United Nations looms increasingly large on the post–cold war Japanese foreign policy agenda. From 1997 until the end of next year, Japan is serving as a nonpermanent member of the United Nations Security Council, thus participating in dealing with post–cold war security issues such as regional conflicts, nonproliferation, terrorism, development, and the global environment and energy. Japan is seeking permanent membership on the Security Council, while seeking reform of the United Nations. Tokyo was disappointed by the November 1997 postponement of a decision on increasing membership.

ECONOMIC AND ENVIRONMENTAL CONTRIBUTIONS   Many Japanese believe that Japan should make significant "nonmilitary" contributions to the welfare of the international community, especially in the form of Official Development Assistance (ODA). The ODA Charter, adopted in June 1992, provides a philosophy of aid, its geographical priorities, and guidelines for implementation, including taking into account conditions in recipient countries in the areas of environmental protection, peaceful use of aid, democratic governance, and human rights. In June 1997, Hashimoto announced the "Initiative for Sustainable Development toward the 21st Century," a comprehensive environmental cooperation policy addressing a variety of problems, including global warming, air and water pollution, waste disposal, deforestation, and loss of marine and terrestrial biodiversity. Japan's environmental aid already has been quite substantial. In the five-year period beginning in fiscal 1992, its environmental ODA has grown to ¥1.44 trillion (US$11 billion). At the December 1997 third Conference of Parties of the UN Framework Convention on Climate Change, held in Kyoto, Japan announced the "Kyoto Protocol," which focused on assisting developing countries combat global warming.

Nonetheless, dire financial conditions in Japan and the weaker yen have forced Japan to cut its ODA budget substantially. Japan's ODA in fiscal 1996 fell from the previous year for the first time since 1990, though Japan retained its position as the world's largest donor. In 1997, the Japanese government decided to cut the fiscal 1998 ODA budget by 10 percent. Japan also decided to cut the fiscal 1998 budget for UN organizations, including the High Commissioner for Refugees.

UN PEACEKEEPING OPERATIONS AND HUMANITARIAN INTERNATIONAL RELIEF ACTIVITIES   Since the International Peace and Cooperation Law was enacted in August 1992, Japan has been participating in UN peacekeeping operations and international relief activities. In addition to its financial contributions to UN peacekeeping operations and other activities such as humanitarian and refugee assistance in the former Yugoslavia, Japan has lent personnel for UN peacekeeping operations in Angola, Cambodia, Mozambique, El Salvador, and the Golan Heights and for humanitarian assistance activities in the former Zaire.

The issue of Japan's contributions to UN peacekeeping operations has been highly controversial in Japanese domestic politics as Article 9 of the Constitution stipulates that "Japanese people forever renounce war as a sovereign right of the nation and the threat or use of force as a means of settling international disputes." The government, therefore, set five conditions for its participation in UN peacekeeping operations. These are (1) a cease-fire must be in place; (2) the parties to the conflict must have given their consent to the operation; (3) maintenance of neutrality; (4) should any of the conditions (1) to (3) cease to be satisfied, Japan may withdraw its contingent; and (5) use of weapons shall be limited to the minimum necessary for self-protection. Furthermore, Japan's peacekeeping operations are limited only to logistic support assignments such as medical care, transportation, communications and construction services, and the so-called assignments of the core units of peacekeeping forces, such as monitoring disarmament, stationing, and patrol, are to be "frozen" until new legislation is enacted. The government is currently reviewing some of these restrictions so that Japan can more actively participate in UN peacekeeping operations and international relief activities. In 1997, only 45 members of Japan's SDF were engaged in UN peacekeeping operations on the Golan Heights.

7 Republic of Korea

The Security Environment

DOMESTIC DEVELOPMENTS   Two major domestic developments toward the end of 1997 will have a decisive effect on politics in the Republic of Korea and its foreign and defense policies. The first is the full-blown crisis that enveloped South Korea's highly leveraged economy, nearly plunging the country into default at the end of the year. The second is the victory of long-time opposition leader Kim Dae Jung in the December 18 presidential election, marking the first time in the past 36 years that an opposition leader won the presidency.

The South Korean economy had been troubled for some time before the lack of currency reserves forced the government to seek an International Monetary Fund (IMF) bailout package in November. The country's long-time current and trade deficits had begun to lessen in 1997, but confidence in the economy fell following the spectacular corporate failures of Kia Motors and Hanbo Steel. The financial crisis that began in Southeast Asia had a delayed impact on South Korea partly because of the country's currency controls, but it invited the closer scrutiny of the international financial markets to the overextended nature of corporate debt in South Korea. International banks, particularly those in Japan, began to withdraw credit, and the precipitous fall of the won doubled the payment burdens in dollar or yen terms. Even the US$57 billion November agreement with the IMF had little immediate impact on the crisis. With its reserves virtually exhausted, South Korea would have defaulted by the end of the year but for last minute emergency assistance extended by the international financial institutions and some governments and the heavy pressure placed by the European, Japanese, and U.S. governments on their banks to roll over short-term loans and begin a process of converting them into manageable long-term instruments.

By the beginning of 1998, it appeared that South Korea might weather the crisis, but at the sacrifice of at least two to three years of slow economic growth and unemployment of as much as 4 percent to 6 percent—very high by historical South Korean standards. Aside from its economic impact, the major effect of the crisis was psychological, as years of highly successful performance had given the South Korean people a strong sense of self-confidence. This was reflected not only in the ambitious expansion programs of the South Korean *chaebol* but also in President Kim Young Sam's "globalization" policy, which included a successful campaign to join the Organization for Economic Cooperation and Development, a "rich man's club." The economic collapse put an end to South Korean hubris and threatened the underlying social contract, including the promise of lifelong employment, that has been an important part of the South Korean success story. The new president's first challenge lies in restoring a sense of hope and optimism to the South Korean people.

In the midst of the economic emergency, Kim Dae Jung appeared to be the man for the moment. With his history of criticism of the Establishment and his long-established ties with labor, it was hoped that he could gain needed concessions from business and labor for the necessary retrenchments and restructuring. Although Kim only barely won the election with just 40.3 percent of the vote in a three-way race, his postelection support blossomed, giving promise of a strong "honeymoon." Nonetheless, considering the serious economic policy decisions ahead, the continued fractured nature of South Korean politics, and the minority position of his party in the parliament, Kim will need to exercise the utmost political skill to maintain his support base in the year ahead.

THE EXTERNAL SECURITY ENVIRONMENT   South Korean perceptions of a military threat remain dominated by North Korea. As reported in *Asia Pacific Security Outlook 1997,* South Koreans discern three kinds of threat from North Korea: a direct military threat, a diplomatic threat to South Korea's important relationship with the United States, and a potential spillover threat from the uncertain political future of the North due to its own system and its economic and resource problems. During 1997, there was relatively little change in the South Korean assessments of the first two threats, but on the third, some influential analysts believe that the North Korean regime has improved its survival prospects.

According to this viewpoint, the North has been successful in winning the critically needed level of minimum support from abroad without compromising the basis of regime legitimacy in the philosophy of *juche* (self-reliance). It succeeded in increasing its support from a doubtful China by skillfully playing a Taiwan card by concluding a contract to store Taiwanese nuclear waste. And it gained modern nuclear energy technology and food aid from the international community by playing on proliferation fears and humanitarian impulses. Kim Jong Il's success in consolidating his leadership and establishing his legitimacy as his father's heir was demonstrated when in October he formally assumed his father's position as general secretary of the Korean Workers' Party. The dramatic February 1997 defection of North Korean Hwang Jang Yop, an architect of the *juche* ideology, reflected the consolidation of Kim Jong Il's own power base. While the North remains a weak country, an early collapse thus seems less likely. Some South Koreans regretfully regard this as a closing of a possible window of opportunity for achieving the long-desired goal of national reunification. For many others, however, stability in the North is desirable because the South currently is in no economic condition to deal with the consequences of a collapse of order in the North.

South Koreans remain on guard against the formidable military forces of the North and the North's continued efforts to enhance its relations with Japan and the United States at the South's expense. In general, however, the broader Northeast Asian security environment seemed to have improved during 1997. The groundbreaking took place for the North Korean light water reactor facilities under the auspices of the Korean Peninsula Energy Development Organization (KEDO), and South Korean workers are in the North working on this project. In December, the first formal Four-Party Talks to seek a permanent peace mechanism to replace the Korean Armistice Agreement took place in Geneva, thus bringing to fruition a process initiated by President Kim Young Sam and U.S. President Bill Clinton on April 16, 1996. Based on previous experience, the negotiations are likely to drag on for years unless there is some breakthrough in relations between Seoul and Pyongyang. Some South Koreans believe that Kim Dae Jung is more likely to try to initiate a meaningful dialogue with the North and is acceptable to the North as a negotiating partner because of his steadfast opposition to the South's military regimes. In this view, he will give high priority to diplomacy toward the North. Others believe that Kim is unlikely to press such a campaign because he needs to dissociate himself from the North and give full attention to the South's economic problems.

During the year, South Koreans welcomed the improvement in Sino-American relations as a positive feature of the security environment. There was some ambivalence, however, about the new Guidelines for U.S.-Japan Defense Cooperation as they imply a broader regional Japanese military role. Nevertheless, there is a growing feeling among some South Korean defense specialists that a Japanese military role, as long as it is carried out in conjunction with the United States, may be a useful addition to regional and South Korean security.

Unlike other parts of Asia, there is little overt concern in South Korea about a potential threat from China. This reflects the historical and cultural relationship between the two countries. The two countries have no territorial conflict, unlike Japan and South Korea. Some specialists, however, see China as a nonmilitary threat. They point out that because of the nature of its economy, China is South Korea's most formidable economic rival and that China has become the major outside source of maritime and airborne environmental pollution affecting the Korean peninsula.

Defense Policy and Issues

DEFENSE OBJECTIVES   South Korea's defense white paper, which has been published annually since 1988, lists four basic defense objectives: (1) to provide a solid defense posture against any form of North Korean adventurism, (2) to develop security and diplomatic links with other countries to meet the challenges of a changing security environment, (3) to establish a force structure for the needs of the 21st century, including a reunified Korea, and (4) to establish an image of reliable armed forces. This last includes maintaining public trust in the military, regaining support from civilian authorities, and strengthening military morale.

South Korea has been pursuing an increasingly self-reliant military posture. However, the 1953 ROK-U.S. Mutual Defense Treaty remains the main axis for South Korean security, serving to deter aggression from the North, provide a basis for improved South-North relations in the future, and help maintain peace and stability in Northeast Asia as a whole.

DEFENSE SPENDING AND PERSONNEL   Until the recent economic difficulties forced major defense cuts, South Korea's defense budget had been steadily increasing to meet North Korean contingencies and to prepare for a more uncertain political environment in the coming century. At W13.79 trillion (US$8.15 million at US$1=W1,691) in 1997, the defense budget was approximately 3.3 percent of gross national product and 20.2 percent of the national budget in fiscal year 1997.

Of the budget, 71.1 percent was devoted to maintenance, including personnel, equipment, bases, and so forth. The remainder was for improved defense capabilities.

Defense manpower stands at 690,000 personnel, of which 560,000 are in the army, 67,000 in the navy, and 63,000 in the air force.

DEFENSE RESTRUCTURING AND PROCUREMENT   Among the priorities of the Kim Young Sam administration were enhanced transparency and responsibility in defense procurement programs and the establishment of a more professional and streamlined defense structure and personnel management system. Innovations included (1) a defense business office to manage production, procurement, and sales in the Ministry of National Defense, (2) a headquarters under the Joint Chiefs of Staff to evaluate ground, air, and naval force capabilities on an integrated basis, (3) a regular office for monitoring and promoting an ongoing process of military restructuring, and (4) simplification of the command structure.

Procurement efforts acknowledge the increasing importance of air and naval forces in the strategic environment of the 21st century. The 1991 Persian Gulf War and the 1996 Kangnung incident drew attention to the importance of these forces in future contingencies. The latter case involved the discovery of a North Korean midget submarine which brought in North Korean infiltrators, launching an expensive manhunt in eastern South Korea. Defense planners argue that the new environment will be less certain and will involve various kinds of lower-level, offshore threats. In this environment, South Korea will also have to increase its ability to respond to international peacekeeping operations carried out under the mandate of the United Nations.

Because of budgetary problems, South Korea will have to postpone or reconsider some of its proposed purchases, including the AWACS airborne surveillance system and naval helicopters. Another procurement issue arose over South Korea's efforts to diversify weapons sources and, particularly, its interest in Russian weaponry. This resulted in strong protests from the United States, South Korea's traditional supplier.

DEFENSE BURDEN-SHARING   Because of the economic crisis, defense burden-sharing will likely become an issue between South Korea and the United States. There are two dimensions: South Korean support for the U.S. forces and facilities in South Korea and South Korea's very large contribution to KEDO. As for the first, South Korea began paying for South Korean employees and their facilities in 1991, and since that time, South Korea's contribution rose from an initial US$150 million to US$363 million in 1997. Under an agreement reached in 1995, South Korean support was to rise by 10 percent annually from 1996 to 1998, reflecting inflation and South Korea's increased capabilities. Because of the economic crisis, the inflation rate will rise substantially, whereas South Korea's ability to provide support in dollar terms has dropped dramatically. South Korea will also have difficulty with payment for the light water reactors being transferred to the North. Not only is this a major economic burden, but it is one that has become more politically sensitive under the current economic conditions. South Korea will likely raise these issues with the U.S. government and other KEDO partners, seeking relief from the high costs now imposed on it. However, it is anticipated that the U.S. Congress will insist on a continuing high level of South Korean support for both U.S. forces and KEDO.

Contributions to Regional and Global Security

STABILITY IN THE KOREAN PENINSULA   South Korea's most important contribution to regional and global security comes through its efforts to maintain stability in the Korean peninsula. As indicated above, these efforts include not only its deterrent and defense efforts carried out in conjunction with its alliance with the United States but also its diplomatic initiatives, food assistance to the North, and major contribution to the KEDO effort to prevent nuclear proliferation. Spending 3.3 percent of gross national product on defense, South

Korea continues to bear a relatively large defense burden compared with many other Asian countries. Until a change of policy in the North permitting reconciliation and reunification, this burden will continue to be high.

The slow process of engagement of the North in improved bilateral dialogues and multilateral mechanisms has been very frustrating for South Koreans. From 1990 to 1992, eight high-level talks occurred between the two Korean states, culminating in the Joint Declaration on the Denuclearization of the Korean Peninsula in 1991, the February 1992 South-North Korean Agreement on Reconciliation, Cooperation and Exchanges, and the September 1992 "Nonaggression Protocol." In late 1992, citing the ROK-U.S. military exercise "Team Spirit," North Korea withdrew from this bilateral process, and despite numerous efforts to resume confidence building between North and South, the process remains stalled. There remains a strong desire in the government and among the public to resume meaningful bilateral discussions as well as to make progress on a permanent peace agreement through the Four-Party Talks.

INTENSIFIED SECURITY DIALOGUE   Since the end of the 1980s, South Korea has been actively engaged in security cooperation with neighboring countries in an effort to improve the security environment of the peninsula and the region as a whole. These efforts have focused on relations with Japan, China, and Russia. In the South Korean view, the country's efforts over the past decade or more have been successful, witnessing the normalization of relations with both Russia and China as well as the admission of the two Korean states into the United Nations.

With Japan, military cooperation began in 1965. Information and personnel exchanges have been on the rise since 1994 when the South Korean minister of national defense visited Japan for the first time. Other issues, however, have troubled South Korean-Japanese relations. The centuries-old territorial dispute over Tok Do Island (Takeshima Island to the Japanese) has been rekindled in the past two years, following proclamations of the respective nations' exclusive economic zones. South Korea has exercised greater vigilance in the vicinity of Tok Do, which it claims as an integral part of Korea. The air space over the island, for example, is categorized as South Korea's Air Defense Identification Zone. Another sensitive issue arose over the Japanese-Korean fishing agreement, which Japan decided to abrogate in the fall of 1997. At South Korea's request, the announcement of the decision was postponed to January 1998.

Military relations with China have steadily improved since South Korea first assigned a military attaché to its embassy in Beijing in December 1993.

A military attaché office was opened in Moscow in 1991. In 1994, there was an exchange of visits of South Korean and Russian defense ministers. In 1996, when the South Korean defense minister again visited Moscow, a "Memorandum of Understanding" on mutual military cooperation was reached with Russia on November 4. South Korea and Russia also exchange naval visits and hold yearly meetings to prevent accidents at sea.

PARTICIPATION IN UN PEACEKEEPING OPERATIONS In a period of about four to five years, South Korea has made considerable progress in strengthening contributions to UN peacekeeping operations (PKO). Since 1993, 1,300 peacekeepers have been dispatched for UN operations in Somalia, Western Sahara, Angola, Georgia, and India-Pakistan. In March 1995, South Korea made a list of 800 men in six fields to be available on a standby basis to serve in UN peacekeeping operations. If requested by the United Nations, South Korea would participate, taking into account its own security situation and domestic legalities. The Defense Staff College established a peacekeeping operations education system in 1995. About 30 officers have been assigned to the Pearson Peacekeeping Center in Canada, the Polish PKO Academy, and the UN Training Center in Scandinavia. One South Korean lieutenant-colonel is teaching at the Pearson Peacekeeping Center.

ECONOMIC RECOVERY The Korean peninsula has long been a hot spot in regional and global security affairs. In 1997, it also became a hot spot for the world economy. A default in the world's 11th largest economy would have had substantial repercussions for the international banking system and particularly for Japan's sluggish economy, as Japanese banks were the largest lenders to their South Korean counterparts. Thus South Korea's economic recovery may be the country's most important contribution to regional security during the next few years.

For the coming two or three years, South Korea will be more focused on internal recovery. Budgets for international activities, such as Overseas Development Assistance, host nation support for U.S.

forces, intellectual exchange, and international organizations, which had seen rapid increases in recent years, will undoubtedly be substantially reduced in dollar terms. Nonetheless, South Korean recovery will provide a stronger long-term basis for South Korea's contributions to regional and global security.

8 Malaysia

The Security Environment

The year 1997 was dominated by two events that impacted on the country's security environment: East Asia's worst economic crisis and the prolonged haze resulting from Indonesian forest fires. These two developments affected the well-being of Malaysians and posed serious challenges to the security of the state, as comprehensively defined.

The most serious challenge to Malaysia's security was no doubt the regional economic crisis, precipitated by turmoil in some of the region's currencies. Almost unprecedented in the way it hit and has continued to plague the region, the economic crisis had a staggering effect. What began as the floatation of the Thai currency soon ballooned into a regional financial disaster, leaving a trail of battered economies. Several states in the region saw their stock markets plunge and the values of their currencies drastically slashed and found that their private corporations were indebted to foreign lenders to the point of bankruptcy.

Malaysia was not spared from the domino effect of the currency crisis. Like its neighbors, it found itself extremely vulnerable to the vicissitudes of the external environment and unable to resist the economic contagion. Overheating in some sectors of the economy, such as the property market, compounded Malaysia's problems. For a state that has prided itself on years of impressive economic growth and that has declared a vision of attaining developed-nation status by the year 2020—encapsulated in its economic plan of action, Vision 2020—this crisis was a particularly poignant major setback for Malaysia's development efforts. More importantly, it demonstrated that the government was almost powerless to contend with external market forces that were wreaking havoc on the country's economy. Fund managers and currency traders, who once entered the country in droves, dumped the local currency and pulled out of the stock market. Meanwhile, the Malaysian public withdrew huge amounts of money from local banks and transferred it to foreign banks incorporated in the country. While this was short of a total capital flight, it soon became clear that the economic crisis had brought on another critical crisis—a crisis of confidence reaching dangerous proportions.

By November 1997, the government developed an economic package designed to restore confidence in its currency and in its development plans. Measures taken to resuscitate Malaysia's economy included cutting public spending by 18 percent, including a 10 percent cut in the pay of government ministers and other top government officials; reducing the current account deficit to 3 percent of gross national product from the 4-to-5-percent range previously; and revising the 1998 growth forecast to 4 percent from 7 percent previously. The government also announced the deferment of a number of megaprojects, including the controversial multibillion dollar Bakun Dam and the land bridge to Thailand. Another significant step was the formation of the National Economic Action Council, a body charged with formulating measures for economic recovery. Of note is the fact that while a number of strategies were quickly adopted to steer the country out of recession, the government has successfully resisted seeking help from the International Monetary Fund (IMF), which has already come to the rescue of Indonesia, South Korea, and Thailand.

Despite the introduction of such measures, Malaysia's stock and foreign exchange markets had yet to react positively by year's end. Instead, the Malaysian public had come, inevitably, to the realization that economic recovery would be far more difficult to achieve than initially anticipated. This prospect of a difficult, protracted recovery brought to the fore a number of critical issues that have serious repercussions on the security of the state.

One of the most serious problems resulting from the crisis is the rise in unemployment, which is expected to gather momentum in 1998. For the past several years, Malaysia has enjoyed full employment. In fact, for the country to go into full gear with its development projects, particularly in the construction and manufacturing industries, it has had to employ foreign workers. It is estimated that there are 1.2 million legal foreign workers in Malaysia and about 800,000 illegal workers employed mostly in the construction, manufacturing, and agricultural industries. Most of these legal and illegal workers come from Indonesia. With the liquidity crunch, several infrastructure projects had to be postponed or even abandoned, thus leaving thousands of workers jobless. Up to one million foreign workers in Malaysia may need to be sent back to their home countries. Moreover, many more employees from other sectors of the economy also face the prospect of losing their jobs as the crisis continues unabated. The immensity of this problem has just started to unfold as many more companies find themselves unable to survive the mounting debts to both local and foreign banks, the decrease in demand, and lower output. How to absorb jobless workers and what to do with them pose serious challenges to the administration, as large-scale unemployment will certainly threaten social stability and harmony.

While the country gears itself to grapple with rising unemployment, it will also have to contend with an expected influx of even more illegal workers from neighboring countries, in particular Indonesia. How best to handle this problem without causing tensions with neighboring states poses another challenge to the government.

Unemployment and the possibility of again relaxing affirmative action programs to enable the economy to recover more quickly could raise ethnic tensions, which are, nonetheless, unlikely to reach serious levels. The affirmative action programs launched with the New Economic Policy in 1970 had helped to significantly reduce the gap between Bumiputra (indigenous) and non-Bumiputra incomes. The economic recession in the mid-1980s forced the government to relax the programs to expedite recovery, with the result that the gap in ethnic incomes began to widen again, though only marginally.

Another relaxation of these programs can be expected to further widen this gap. Given the present economic downturn, however, relaxation appears unavoidable. The programs' goal of improved income parity among ethnic groups is predicated upon a growing economy. When growth falters, the programs must be moderated. However, as in the mid-1980s, serious ethnic tensions are unlikely, owing to the progress in nation building achieved over the four decades since independence.

At this juncture, it is important to emphasize that the nonmilitary aspects of security have dominated the security concerns of the country. Although the current economic crisis is eroding the public's confidence in the state so vital to maintaining political stability, systemic stresses brought on by the crisis have not yet resulted in political instability in Malaysia. Nevertheless, these stresses are potentially destabilizing if not carefully managed. This underscores the relevance of understanding the integrated nature of security wherein nonmilitary factors (in this case, the regional currency crisis) could trigger a series of events that then seriously threaten the security of states.

This fact is all the more salient when considering the second major event that affected Malaysia in 1997: the protracted thick haze that enveloped the country for about four months beginning in July 1997. A result of the forest fires in Indonesia, the haze affected not only Malaysia but also Singapore and parts of Thailand, and has been described by the World Wide Fund for Nature as "an environmental catastrophe." For the countries most affected, including Malaysia, this disaster resulted in several millions of dollars in lost business. More importantly, analyses of the long-term health implications of the pollution indicate that the haze threatens lives; it also caused severe damage to the ecology. This was not the first time that Malaysia has suffered such a haze problem, but the 1997 haze was the longest and the most severe. Pollution levels in the Malaysian state of Sarawak well exceeded danger indexes, often for days on end. Yet the Malaysian government found itself helpless in mitigating, let alone eliminating, the effects of the haze.

The haze problem further illustrated the transboundary nature of this security threat and the exigency of concerted regional and even global efforts to address the problem. Despite the fact that a mechanism within the Association of Southeast Asian Nations (ASEAN) exists to deal with transboundary pollution, the coordination among those countries most affected was poor. The response to the haze problem also revealed the inadequacy of cooperation between Malaysia (and Singapore) and Indonesia. Instead of getting a quick response from its ASEAN partners, Malaysia received assistance from a number of Western governments, including Canada, France, and the United States. Moreover, while the efforts of firefighters to douse the forest fires in Indonesia (in which Malaysians actively participated) were commendable and brave, they were only marginally effective. Rains rather than government action eventually put out the fires.

These two issues of currencies and haze are concrete examples of a type of problem that transcends boundaries and thus defies solution by traditional means invoking notions of national sovereignty. The borderless nature of such a problem makes it a potential threat to the security of an entire region.

Defense Policy and Issues

Two developments are particularly notable: Malaysia's efforts to strengthen the transparency of defense information, and cutbacks in procurement as a result of the financial crisis. The centerpiece of the first effort is the Ministry of Defense's publication of *Malaysia Defence: Toward Defence Self-Reliance*. Although there have been earlier ministry publications, notably the 1994 *Honour and Sacrifice: The Malaysian Armed Forces*, the current book is the first to comprehensively address national defense policy. Individual chapters deal with the country's strategic outlook, its defense organization, defense science and technology support, and the contribution of the armed forces to global peace. In addition, one chapter addresses the armed forces' relations with the public.

The economic crisis has had a significant impact on defense policy and procurement. The drastic cut in public expenditure has naturally affected the acquisition plans of the armed forces. It appears that a number of procurement programs will be temporarily shelved. These include the army's plan to acquire main battle tanks, as well as attack and transport helicopters for its air wing intended for inclusion in the Rapid Reaction Force. The air force is in a better position, having recently acquired most of its capital equipment, including an earlier purchase of F-18s which arrived in the middle of 1997. However, further augmentation plans, including the upgrading of some weapons systems, may be put on hold. The navy's earlier purchase of Italian corvettes, initially intended for the Iraqi navy, was delivered. The navy also announced that a German shipbuilding consortium was the successful bidder for its Offshore Patrol Vessel program.

Aside from procurement, it can be anticipated that military readiness will be impacted, as the armed forces will have to reduce the number of joint military exercises in line with current budgetary constraints.

Contributions to Regional and Global Security

Malaysian foreign policy was preoccupied during much of the first part of 1997 with the goal of uniting all of Southeast Asia under the ASEAN umbrella (ASEAN-10). The government hoped that the "consummation" of ASEAN would be achieved during the regional association's 30th anniversary celebration, which was being chaired by Malaysia. Although the inclusion of Myanmar proved to be controversial both within and outside the region, the Malaysian government regarded Myanmar's admission as both a logical extension of ASEAN's policy of constructive engagement with the Myanmar government and a positive step toward strengthening international relations in Southeast Asia. The Malaysian government believes that inclusion in ASEAN strengthens the commitment of individual member countries to regional cooperation and thus is a constructive step toward a more peaceful regional order. It would seem, then, that ASEAN's decision during the July 1997 ASEAN Ministerial Meeting to admit Myanmar could be considered a victory for Malaysia's diplomacy and a reflection of its growing influence in the region.

At the global level, Malaysia remains one of Asia's most active participants in UN peacekeeping operations. It is anticipated that Malaysia's current peacekeeping commitments to war-torn countries such as Bosnia-Herzegovina and Somalia will not be drastically affected by its financial difficulties. However, Malaysia is unlikely to be able to embark upon new commitments in the near future.

The economic crisis and the country's response to it will continue to dominate the security concerns of Malaysia. Yet, while Malaysia grapples with this problem it will continue to be actively committed to regional stability. Toward the end of 1997, Kuala Lumpur hosted a summit of the enlarged ASEAN group with China, Japan, and South Korea. Malaysia also contributed US$1 billion to both Indonesia and Thailand as part of the international efforts, led by the IMF, to help these countries. Malaysia's main contribution to regional stability, however, will be through its own adjustment to the crisis.

9 New Zealand

The Security Environment

New Zealand's regional security outlook is optimistic. There is no sense of a direct military threat. There is a remarkable consensus among New Zealand political parties, commentators, and government officials that trade is important, regional stability is indispensable, and New Zealand should be actively involved in peacekeeping. There is also agreement that the security of Australia, the Southwest Pacific, and East Asia is important to New Zealand. Critics contend that more emphasis should be given to developing defense relationships with nontraditional partners. Where there is disagreement is on the role of defense. The main dividing line is between the "internationalists," who support full diplomatic and military engagement in global and regional security activities, and the "reductionists," who favor the restricting of defense engagement to peacekeeping operations and civic assistance mainly in the Southwest Pacific. Internationalists tend to be drawn from the political center. Reductionists represent an unlikely confluence of new left and new right opinion bound by the view that defense spending should be dramatically reduced.

There is recognition among mainstream politicians, commentators, and officials that regional relationships are changing, and a general consensus exists that the new shape of these relationships has yet to be worked out. Only fringe commentators from the new right boldly assert that the market will create security. From the new left, the minority view is expressed that war between states has ended.

WHITE PAPER   The New Zealand government's perspective on regional security is well expressed in the defense white paper published in November 1997. More emphasis is placed in this white paper than in others on interdependence in the region. The white paper observes that it is too soon to know whether economic prosperity and the interdependence it has created may make future wars less likely. The costs of future troubles are forecast to be high, and the new interdependence means that these costs will be carried not just by the countries that are in dispute.

The government and commentators alike appreciate that the working out of relationships between China, Japan, and the United States will, more than anything else, determine the levels of confidence and security in the region. The government supports the U.S. forward presence and role in the region, which are viewed as being generally welcomed by other states. Japan's reaffirmation of its continuing security alliance with the United States and the development of new U.S.-Japan security guidelines are supported by the government. However, critics point to the risks of strengthening military alliances without an enemy in mind, and to the fact that China is understandably unsettled by the expansion of alliances around its Pacific borders led by the United States.

The white paper reflects the mainstream New Zealand view that the principal new element in the region's strategic equation is the rapid rise in the economic importance of China. China's role as a major power in the region is welcomed and will require an adjustment in the existing structure of regional relationships. There is general agreement in New Zealand that it is important that other states work closely with China to ensure that its aspirations and new weight are accommodated as smoothly as possible.

The Association of Southeast Asian Nations (ASEAN) is regarded as a fourth regional power by New Zealand officials. ASEAN's influence on other regional powers on issues as varied as the South China Sea, Cambodia, and human rights is generally interpreted in positive terms by commentators and officials alike.

THREATS   Security analysts and officials emphasize that the rash of insurgency movements, which threatened several states following World War II, has all but vanished. The persistence of underlying tensions and disputed boundaries is acknowledged, although both commentators and officials concur that sound diplomacy can manage these problems. Officials regard the Korean peninsula as the immediate exception to the generally favorable security environment, with an unpredictable risk of war in the short term. Opinion among commentators on this subject is divided. Looking to the longer term, there is a general consensus that the major regional security issue is the future of Taiwan.

The 1997 stock market and currency crises that affected most of East Asia were followed closely in New Zealand, largely from the economic perspective. In general, the stock market and currency crises were regarded by government and economic commentators as necessary market readjustments caused by overvalued currencies, inflated stock markets, and weak financial systems, and to a lesser extent as the consequence of speculative investments in property. A short-term lowering of demand for New Zealand exports (40 percent of New Zealand's trade is with East Asia) is anticipated. Tourism from East Asia may slow. However, New Zealanders will benefit from the declining price of imports from East Asian countries.

New Zealand opinion is not unduly concerned over the issue of arms modernization in Asia. Left-wing commentators and peace groups consider that a regional arms race is taking place, but they also argue that the prospects of war are slight. Mainstream commentators, officials, and the government interpret regional arms acquisitions to be largely the outcome of prosperity and the development of outward-looking strategic orientations among Asian countries. The trend toward a capacity to project power beyond national borders is noted, but discussion of this issue is generally limited to specialist defense commentators and defense officials.

Defense Policies and Issues

DEFENSE SPENDING AND FORCE STRUCTURE   New Zealand currently spends NZ$1.2 billion (US$696 million at NZ$1.00 = US$0.58) a year on defense, which is 1.3 percent of gross domestic product. The budget decline of 33 percent in real terms since 1989–90 is arrested by the white paper with an increase of NZ$650 million (US$377 million) over five years.

The white paper emphasizes the importance of maintaining a modern, interoperable, and effective defense force. The white paper signaled the government's commitment to a long-term reequipment funding program for the New Zealand Defense Force. In essence, the structure of the Defense Force is to remain constant, although its capacity is to be upgraded and modernized. The major change is the reshaping of the navy combat force from four to three frigates.

The white paper provides funding for the two regular infantry battalions to be brought to full strength, the acquisition of new armored vehicles, radios, direct-fire support weapons, night observation systems, and medium-range antiarmor systems. The antisubmarine and maritime surveillance force will be modernized. The option of buying a third Australia-New Zealand Army Corps (ANZAC) frigate is kept open. Long-term funds are identified to replace Hercules transport aircraft and fast jets.

Reaction to the white paper varied. General media reaction was positive. Opposition political parties criticized the paper for its alleged preoccupation with the past. Peace groups objected to the internationalist and regional outlook and the justification of modern warships and fast jet aircraft.

DOCTRINE   New Zealand Defense Force doctrine is an adaptation of the doctrine of allies and friends such as Australia, the United Kingdom, and the United States. It provides that the armed forces must be trained and equipped for both conventional and peacekeeping roles, and must be able to operate in lower and higher levels of intensity of conflict. Emphasis is placed on interoperability with ABCA (America, Britain, Canada and Australia Agreement) standards.

The implications of military modernization, which are a major focus of attention by the Australian, U.K., and U.S. militaries (especially precision-guided weapons, information warfare, and the concept of dominant engagement), are being investigated by the New Zealand Defense Force and the Ministry of Defense.

PEACEKEEPING   The defense white paper emphasizes that although there will be an enduring demand for low-level peacekeeping, especially in missions where protagonists have exhausted themselves, peacekeepers will need to be prepared to operate in increasingly dangerous operations launched during hostilities. The white paper argues that because New Zealand forces are likely to encounter protagonists armed with lethal weapons systems such as portable anti-tank, air, and ship missiles, and relatively modern artillery and armor, the New

Zealand Defense Force will need to be prepared for operations that may escalate quickly to higher levels of intensity.

CONTRIBUTIONS TO REGIONAL AND GLOBAL SECURITY

PARTNERSHIP WITH AUSTRALIA   Despite some frictions in the relationship (largely over Australian criticism of New Zealand's defense effort), there is a general consensus among mainstream political opinion and commentators that Australia is New Zealand's closest and most important security partner. The New Zealand Defense Force could add one-fifth to the capability of the Australian Defense Force.

At the heart of New Zealand-Australian defense cooperation is the Closer Defense Relations agreement. The purpose of the agreement is to increase the effectiveness of the defense forces of both countries through consultative decision-making, complementarity and interoperability, and consultation over long-term planning.

NEW ZEALAND AND THE UNITED STATES   Although Wellington endorses the leading role of the United States in Asia Pacific regional security, New Zealand's own defense relationship with the United States is still dominated by Washington's reaction to New Zealand legislation in the 1980s banning nuclear-armed and nuclear-powered vessels and aircraft from New Zealand. Nevertheless, New Zealand forces have worked with the U.S. military forces on numerous operations in recent years, including the 1991 Persian Gulf War and peace support activities such as the Multinational Interception Force in the Persian Gulf, the Multinational Force and Observers in the Sinai, and in Somalia, Rwanda, and Haiti.

There is frustration at the highest levels of the New Zealand government, and among mainstream commentators, with the U.S. refusal to restore full defense cooperation. New Zealanders also resent criticism of New Zealand by U.S. officials for low defense spending. In Wellington it is seen as inconsistent for Washington to call for New Zealand to increase defense spending but still be unwilling to exercise or train together.

Although this "unfinished business" has strained New Zealand's defense relations with Washington, both sides now regard each other as good friends. The United States is prepared to sell New Zealand defense equipment and to cooperate closely on technical standardization issues. The suspension by the United States of all high-level diplomatic and political contact between the two countries has been lifted.

THE BOUGAINVILLE PEACE PROCESS New Zealand has played the leading role in brokering talks between participants to the conflict in Bougainville, at the invitation of the government of Papua New Guinea and the Bougainville rebels themselves. (See the discussion of the Bougainville situation in the Papua New Guinea chapter.)

A major event in 1997 was the signing by officials from the Papua New Guinea government and representatives from the rebel factions of the Burnham Truce (named after the New Zealand army base at which negotiations were held). The agreement established a Truce Monitoring Group of unarmed military and civilian personnel, drawn mostly from New Zealand but including members from Australia, Fiji, Tonga, and Vanuatu and led by a New Zealand army officer with an Australian deputy. The group is a neutral body designed to help reduce tensions on the island, build trust, and discourage potential breaches of the truce.

The truce was followed by the signing of the Lincoln Agreement (named after the university in Christchurch that was the site of discussions) by the parties to the conflict on January 23, 1998. The Lincoln Agreement extends the truce to April 30, 1998, after which a permanent cease-fire is to come into effect. UN Security Council endorsement of these arrangements is to be sought by the Papua New Guinea government, including the appointment of a special observing mission to monitor arrangements. The Lincoln Agreement includes provisions that cover the withdrawal of the Papua New Guinea Defense Force from the island, the restoration of civil authority, and mechanisms to solicit aid for reconstruction. The parties agreed to meet again in Bougainville before the end of 1998 to address the political future of the island.

DEFENSE COOPERATION WITH SINGAPORE AND MALAYSIA New Zealand, along with Singapore, Malaysia, Australia, and Britain, is a member of the Five Power Defense Arrangements (FPDA) dating from 1971 and reinvigorated in recent years at the initiative of Singapore and Malaysia. Under the FPDA, in the event of an attack or threat directed against either Singapore or Malaysia, the member governments would "immediately consult together for the purpose of deciding what measures would be taken jointly or separately." The FPDA uses joint exercises to build trust and to develop and test operational effectiveness. New Zealand contributed two frigates, the operational diving team, and RNZAF Skyhawk and Orion aircraft in the FPDA FLYING FISH exercise in the South China Sea April 13–30, 1997.

At the bilateral level, the New Zealand navy, army, and air force regularly exercise with their Singaporean and Malaysian counterparts. In 1995, a New Zealand-Singapore Defense Cooperation Group was formed to oversee at the senior officials level the implementation, coordination, and management of defense activities between the two countries (including exercising in New Zealand by Singapore army medium artillery). A nearly identical group was formed with Malaysia in the same year.

THE DEFENSE MUTUAL ASSISTANCE PROGRAM (MAP) MAP provides assistance to security and paramilitary forces in the South Pacific and Southeast Asia, including Fiji, Tonga, the Cook Islands, Niue, Western Samoa, Vanuatu, the Solomon Islands, Papua New Guinea, Malaysia, Singapore, Thailand, Brunei, the Philippines, and Indonesia. MAP activities are coordinated with Australian and U.S. counterparts. Approximately 235 Pacific and 70 Asian students are trained annually in New Zealand. On average, just under 40 in-country instructor teams are deployed in the Pacific and 12 to Southeast Asia each year.

New Zealand's defense links with Northeast Asia are growing. New Zealand exercised with the South Korean navy for the first time in 1997. New Zealand has a long-standing dialogue on security issues with Japan, and both countries have exchanged ship visits for many years. Security dialogues are becoming more frequent with South Korea and China. Resident defense attachés will be appointed in Beijing and Seoul within a year.

REGIONAL COOPERATION AND DIALOGUES New Zealand is deeply committed to the regional dialogue processes and is sympathetic and supportive of the constructive role being taken by the states of ASEAN. New Zealand is a dialogue partner to ASEAN and an inaugural member of the ASEAN Regional Forum (ARF). New Zealand participates in the ASEAN Post-Ministerial Conferences and in all ARF meetings. New Zealand cochaired with Thailand the ARF Inter-Sessional Group on Disaster Relief held in Wellington in February 1997. New Zealand also participates in the Council for Security Cooperation in Asia Pacific process.

New Zealand is also a founding member of the South Pacific Forum, a subregional grouping of states and microstates of the Southwest Pacific. New Zealand participates in South Pacific Forum dialogue processes and contributes resources to fisheries surveillance and management programs as well as provides advice and resources to programs dealing with public sector management and reform, environmental protection, and development.

New Zealand is an active participant in the Asia-Pacific Economic Cooperation (APEC) forum, and will chair APEC in 1999. New Zealand has appointed members to the APEC Business Advisory Council to provide linkages to the private sector. New Zealand participates in meetings of the Pacific Economic Cooperative Council.

HUMAN RIGHTS   There is a major division between the government and both left-wing politicians and human rights groups over the role New Zealand should take on human rights issues in East Timor and Myanmar. The government in general favors a quiet dialogue. In contrast, interest groups seek to elevate human rights to the center of bilateral relations between New Zealand and Indonesia and Myanmar. Commentators are split on this issue.

ARMS CONTROL   New Zealand is a strong proponent of nuclear disarmament. Partly in reaction to French nuclear testing at Mururoa Atoll from the 1960s to 1986, opposition to nuclear testing has become a mainstream attitude across the political spectrum.

Non-nuclear legislation passed in 1987 prohibits nuclear vessels (armed/powered) in New Zealand's territorial sea. New Zealand originated the proposal for a South Pacific Nuclear Free Zone and promotes the establishment of political links between nuclear free zones, which now cover the major part of the Southern Hemisphere. New Zealand is a strong supporter of the Comprehensive Test Ban Treaty, the Chemical Weapons Convention, and the Nuclear Non-Proliferation Treaty. It became a full member of the Conference on Disarmament in 1996, and in late 1996 began a two-year term on the Board of Governors of the International Atomic Energy Agency. New Zealand promotes the total ban on antipersonnel mines.

PEACEKEEPING   New Zealand continues to be one of the top five contributors to peacekeeping operations, an impressive record for a small country. It currently participates in nine activities. It contributes seven observers to the UN Truce Supervision Organization, five observers and 12 demining instructors to the UN Angola Verification Mission, two mine action staff to the Cambodian Mine Action Center, 14 operations and logistics staff to the UN Special Commission on Iraq, which investigates Iraq's program of weapons of mass destruction, three officers to the UN Headquarters in New York, seven observers to the UN military observers to the former Yugoslavia, seven officers to the Stabilization Force in the former Yugoslavia, two advisers to the UN Mozambique Demining Operation, and 16 instructors and logistics staff to the Multinational Force and Observers in the Sinai.

The Truce Monitoring Group for Bougainville represents New Zealand's largest military operation since the Vietnam War. Bougainville peacekeeping operations directly absorb 250–300 personnel. The New Zealand contribution, which varies according to need, includes helicopters, Hercules transport aircraft, numerous vehicles and command centers, a frigate, a naval tanker, a diving support ship, and special forces.

10 Papua New Guinea

The Security Environment

As a small country fragmented by geography and ethnicity, the Papua New Guinea state has faced substantial challenges. With a rapidly growing population of almost four million and some 800 separate languages, the country lacks a strong tradition of political organization beyond the village community and temporary alliances of common language (*wantok*) groups. Although the essentially Westminster-style governmental institutions created in the latter stages of colonial rule have proved generally robust, they have been seen by many as a fragile basis for stable democratic government.

In assessing Papua New Guinea's external security outlook, a 1996 defense white paper observed that the country's geographic location puts it in one of the least troubled areas in the world, and that the country's foreign policy of "selective engagement" had produced friendly and productive relations with its neighbors. Nevertheless, the white paper identified as possible challenges Papua New Guinea's relations with the Solomon Islands and issues arising from the resumption of nuclear testing (now terminated) by France in French Polynesia. It noted Papua New Guinea's vulnerability to intrusions into its air and maritime space (particularly through illegal fishing by foreign vessels), and to "illicit activities" such as arms smuggling and drug trafficking.

The existence in the neighboring Indonesian province of Irian Jaya of a Melanesian separatist movement, Organisasi Papua Merdeka (OPM), creates a continuing potential for difficulties in relations with Indonesia. OPM freedom fighters have occasionally sought refuge in the dense jungle on Papua New Guinea's side of the border, and the Indonesian military has periodically pursued OPM sympathizers across Papua New Guinea's border. In 1986, the two countries signed a Treaty of Mutual Respect, Friendship and Cooperation, which addressed their common security concerns and codified arrangements for border management and liaison. Relations have improved in recent years, to the point where several border incursions by Indonesian troops have gone largely unreported. However, the possibility of large-scale migration into Papua New Guinea from areas of Irian Jaya affected by the severe 1997 drought may place new strains on this cooperative relationship.

While the external security environment is seen as generally benign, the defense white paper expressed "major concern" over the internal security situation. Specific concerns included increased problems of law and order, the escalation of land compensation disputes, and the possibility of "uncontrolled ethnic and secessionist movements" along the lines of the Bougainville separatist insurgency.

THE BOUGAINVILLE REBELLION AND THE "SANDLINE AFFAIR"
The most serious internal threat has been the long-running separatist rebellion in Bougainville Province. Dating from 1988, the conflict originated in a dispute over the distribution of returns from the giant Panguna copper mine between local interests, the provincial government, and the central government. However, other elements, including splits among local groups and the inability of the central government to control its security forces, compounded and prolonged the conflict. A number of attempts at negotiated solutions over the years failed or broke down for various reasons. The conflict also led to strains in relations between Papua New Guinea and the neighboring Solomon Islands government.

Prime Minister Julius Chan's frustration and impatience over the Bougainville stalemate, compounded by the prospect of national elections in mid-1997, led to the signing of a US$36 million contract with international military consultant Sandline International. The purpose of the contract was to move against the leadership of the Bougainville Revolutionary Army and ultimately capture the Panguna mine. The Papua New Guinea Defense Force (PNGDF) commander, Brigadier General Jerry Singirok, initially went along with the Sandline proposal, but after it was made public in the Australian press in February 1997 he had a change of heart. On March 17, 1997, speaking on national radio, Singirok announced that he had "canceled all further activities" involving the PNGDF and Sandline, saying, "It is my professional and ethical view that it is wrong to hire Sandline International to carry out the operations on Bougainville." He called on the prime minister, the deputy prime minister, and the defense minister to resign immediately. He also announced that soldiers from the recently formed Special Forces Unit (SFU) had detained the Sandline personnel, who were subsequently deported.

Singirok's actions precipitated what many saw as the most serious political crisis the country has faced since independence. Chan responded by dismissing Singirok, accusing him of "gross insubordination bordering on treason." But there was wide support for the commander. On March 25, with angry crowds surrounding the National Parliament, members of parliament rejected a motion calling on the prime minister and his two colleagues to resign. But the following day the three agreed to "step aside" pending the outcome of an inquiry into the Sandline contract. Then at the end of May, with the inquiry's report still under consideration by the acting prime minister, Chan, claiming that the report cleared him of wrongdoing, announced that he had resumed office.

Popular resentment over the "Sandline affair" was reflected in the outcome of the June 1997 national election. For the first time in a Papua New Guinea election, the incumbent prime minister lost his seat. The defense minister also lost his seat. The incoming government set up a new Sandline inquiry (which had not yet reported as of the end of 1997). Singirok was charged with sedition over his actions in March, and several SFU officers involved in the move against Sandline faced court martial.

Paradoxically, the Sandline affair, popularly denounced largely because of opposition to using foreign mercenaries against Bougainvilleans, became a catalyst in reviving negotiations between the government and the rebels. A New Zealand initiative supported by the Australian government led to new talks, first in New Zealand in July and October 1997, and then in Cairns in November. The negotiations resulted in the signing in October of a truce (the Burnham Truce) and a commitment to a formal meeting of Papua New Guinea and Bougainville leaders by January 1998. In mid-November, a planned 250-strong unarmed Truce Monitoring Group began arriving in Bougainville. The group consisted of around 140 New Zealand troops and civilians, some 90 civilians and troops from Australia, and smaller numbers of personnel from Fiji, Tonga, and Vanuatu, under the command of a senior New Zealand army officer.

The situation on Bougainville remains well short of resolution. Nevertheless, relations between the rebels and the national government (and specifically the security forces) appear to be better than at any time since 1989, and the peace process has gained significant momentum. Also, following the election of a new government in the Solomon Islands in mid-1997, relations between the two Melanesian countries have improved.

LAW, ORDER, AND STATE CAPACITY   To a significant extent, the Bougainville situation has reflected broader problems of public order and state capacity in Papua New Guinea. "Tribal fighting" and criminal activities by so-called *raskol* gangs have been on the increase since the 1970s, resulting in the declaration of a state of emergency in five highlands provinces as early as 1979. There are also fears that an increasingly sophisticated criminal element is establishing linkages with organized crime outside Papua New Guinea, exporting cannabis and stolen vehicle parts and importing firearms. More recently, violence has spread to politics. In both national and local elections in 1997, there were widespread reports of polling irregularities, including intimidation of candidates and voters and bribery. Although such reports are not new, with increasing numbers of candidates and declining margins of victory such behavior can undermine the legitimacy of the electoral process. Videotapes given to the Australian Broadcasting Corporation in late 1997 by a former associate of incoming prime minister Bill Skate implicate Skate (a self-confessed former *raskol*) in allegations of bribery and violence.

The Royal Papua New Guinea Constabulary clearly lacks the capacity to contain the lawlessness, and on a number of occasions has itself resorted to violence, resulting in compensation claims against the state. At the end of 1997, the combined effects of drought and frost—which left more than 600,000 people in a life-threatening situation—placed still further demands on the state's limited capacity to deliver services and contain growing social tensions.

Defense Policy and Issues

In the years preceding independence, there was a good deal of discussion among Papua New Guinea's emerging national leaders as to whether the independent state should maintain a defense force. Some saw a relatively well-provisioned and cohesive military as a possible future threat to democratic government. It was ultimately decided to maintain a defense force separate from the police constabulary. The principle of subordination of the military to the civil authority was established in the Constitution and emphasized in military training. In effect, the PNGDF was maintained in essentially the form in which it had been inherited from Australia. It has continued to receive support through the Australian government's Defense Cooperation Program, but has also signed status of forces agreements or memoranda of understanding with Indonesia, Israel, Malaysia, New Zealand, and the United States.

Foremost among the functions of the PNGDF listed in the Constitution is the defense of Papua New Guinea, although it seems to have been generally accepted that, if the country were attacked, the force could do little more than mount a holding operation awaiting assistance from Australia and other allies. The PNGDF's role also included provision of assistance to the civilian authorities.

In practice, the PNGDF's external role to date has largely consisted of patrolling the borders with Indonesia (to deny access to the OPM) and later the Solomon Islands (to prevent the movement of the Bougainville Revolutionary Army between Bougainville and the Solomon Islands), and policing the waters of its 200-mile economic zone against illegal fishing.

Starting in 1984, the PNGDF has been called upon increasingly to assist the civil authorities in maintaining law and order. The beginning of the armed rebellion on Bougainville in 1988 led to more substantial and continuous involvement in internal security operations.

Persistent over-budget spending by the Defense Department, largely as a result of the Bougainville operation, and its inability to pay allowances due to service personnel have strained relations between the PNGDF and the government. A 10-year program to reorganize force structure, increase force size (from around 4,000 to 5,200 in 1995), and replace major equipment was drawn up in 1988 but did not receive cabinet approval until 1991 and was never implemented. A report prepared in 1991, entitled *Security for Development*, observed that "the most serious, foreseeable threats facing Papua New Guinea are internal" and recommended that the PNGDF's priorities be reordered. A law and order program presented with the 1993 budget proposed to cut force size and place primary emphasis on civic action work. However, like the 1991 plan, this also was not implemented.

The 1996 defense white paper was submitted to the National Parliament in the middle of the year. The white paper argued the need to develop a Papua New Guinean military doctrine and outlined a "*Banis* [perimeter defense] strategy," with particular focus on managing the country's borders, preserving its natural resources, and monitoring and policing its territory. Five major components of the strategy were identified:

- Rationalization of the PNGDF force structure into a small, versatile, mobile force;
- Expansion of Defense Force relations with neighboring countries;
- Decentralization, to give the PNGDF a strategic presence in each of the country's four administrative regions;
- Strengthening the PNGDF's capability to deal with internal security, in part through closer cooperation with the Royal Papua New Guinea Constabulary; and
- Greater emphasis on nation building and development through a variety of measures, including a revitalized Defense Civic Action Program ("*Halipim Progrem*") in conjunction with provincial governments.

As of the end of 1997, in an environment of financial stringency compounded by the fallout from the Sandline affair and a change of government, little progress had been made toward the implementation of the recommendations of the white paper. Morale within the PNGDF remained generally low. The events of early 1997 had also raised questions about longer-term relations between the PNGDF and the civilian government.

Contributions to Regional and Global Security

Papua New Guinea's geographic location makes it a link between Asia and the Pacific. This is reflected in the active role it plays both in the South Pacific Forum and as a member of the "Spearhead Group" of Melanesian countries, and as a signatory to the ASEAN Treaty of Amity and Cooperation and a participant in the Asia-Pacific Economic Cooperation forum and the ASEAN Regional Forum. In 1996, Papua New Guinea's foreign minister proposed to the ASEAN Ministerial Meeting that Papua New Guinea become a permanent associate member.

The 1996 defense white paper supported the idea of collective security arrangements "to enable regional countries to act cohesively toward common security problems." It recommended the establishment of defense relations with Tonga, Fiji, and members of the Melanesian Spearhead Group as a "stepping stone" toward regional security cooperation. It supported establishing a mechanism for discussing regional security concerns and the formation of a regional peacekeeping force. The white paper also endorsed confidence-building measures and transparency in defense policy and military matters.

Papua New Guinea's bilateral relations with the Solomon Islands and Indonesia were strengthened in 1997. Relations with the Solomon Islands, strained since the Bougainville conflict began, improved during the year following a visit to Papua New Guinea by the new Solomon Islands prime minister, Bart Ulufa'alu. In a communiqué, the two governments reaffirmed their common interests, referring specifically to the future possibility of a Melanesian confederation. (However, Ulufa'alu later queried the legality of a border agreement signed by a caretaker government prior to his election.) The Solomon Islands was represented at the Bougainville peace talks in late 1997. On Papua New Guinea's Indonesian border, representatives of the Irian Jaya (Indonesia) and Western (Papua New Guinea) provincial administrations agreed on measures to counter the activities of the OPM and strengthen bilateral commercial and diplomatic ties.

For the near term, the most direct and meaningful contribution that Papua New Guinea could make to improving the regional security environment would be a resolution of the Bougainville conflict. At the end of 1997, this was being actively pursued by the Papua New Guinea government in collaboration with its regional neighbors. Significant participation by Papua New Guinea in wider regional security cooperation will have to await the consolidation of its internal security situation and the strengthening of the structure and capabilities of its own security forces.

11 The Philippines

THE SECURITY ENVIRONMENT

The security outlook of the Philippines in 1997 was fundamentally determined by the need to strengthen domestic polity and by regional developments, especially the growing power of China and the projection of Chinese power in the South China Sea. At the domestic level, efforts were directed toward achieving reconciliation with dissident groups and confronting nonconventional threats to security. Externally, the resurgence of China as the biggest power in the East Asian region and the ambiguity of its policies in the South China Sea conflict continued to cause the Philippine government to be concerned about its territorial and maritime security.

DOMESTIC SECURITY   On the domestic scene, the most prominent political issue was the question of whether President Fidel Ramos could be reelected. Those who supported the president, or fear new leadership, sought to amend the Constitution to permit more than one term. They were opposed by a coalition of political, church, academic, business, student, labor, and nongovernmental organization leaders. Given the history of the Marcos period, many of these groups regarded the effort to change the one-term limit as a threat to the consolidation of the democratic system itself, and in this sense a security threat. Ramos at first was ambiguous about his intentions, but he ultimately announced that he would not challenge the Constitution.

Major breakthroughs in national reconciliation occurred in 1996 and 1997. The first was the signing of the final Peace Agreement with the Moro National Liberation Front (MNLF), on September 2, 1996, and the second was the forging of the cease-fire agreement and commencement of peace talks with the Moro Islamic Liberation Front (MILF). The MNLF and the MILF are both Muslim secessionist movements long operating in the southern Philippines. Following the September 1996 accord, the Southern Philippines Council for Peace and Development was created to implement the agreement, and the Joint Monitoring Committee was established to oversee this implementation. Also as a result of the peace process, the MNLF began integrating into the Armed Forces of the Philippines (AFP). As of August 1997, 893 candidates were undergoing military training. Some believe this integration may pose a problem for the military in the future, considering the differences in mind-sets and tactical orientations of the former insurgents and the present military.

The triumphant feeling over national reconciliation increased when the MILF and the government reached a cease-fire agreement on July 18, 1997. So far, according to military reports, the cease-fire is holding with no confrontations between the MILF and AFP forces. Both parties have agreed to commence negotiations on terms for a permanent peace agreement. The MILF's agenda includes issues relating to land ownership, human rights, economic inequality, and war victims.

These achievements do not necessarily mean a complete or lasting peace in the Philippines' long-troubled Muslim areas. The Abu Sayyaf Group (ASG), a third Mindanao-based Muslim group, remains outside the reconciliation process. The ASG claims responsibility for terrorist activities and to have links with terrorist movements in other Islamic societies. According to Defense Secretary Fortunato Abat, who had headed the peace talks with the MNLF, the Ramos administration cannot negotiate with the ASG on the same terms as with the MNLF or the MILF. He stressed that the ASG is responsible for purely criminal activities for which it must be held accountable.

Over the longer term, the crucial test of the success of the Mindanao peace process will be the ability of the government to address the deplorable socioeconomic conditions of the Muslims, which many believe to be at the root of the Muslim secessionist movement.

On another front, after a year of stalled negotiations, the Ramos administration resumed informal consultations and formal talks with the National Democratic Front (NDF), the political arm of the Communist Party of the Philippines (CPP), in the Netherlands in June 1996. The military estimated in 1996 that the movement's military arm, the

New People's Army, controlled 480 villages, down 94 percent from 8,496 in 1988; had 6,300 insurgent regulars, down 76 percent from 25,800 in 1988; and possessed 5,408 firearms, down 65 percent from 15,500 in 1988. Despite this success, the government wanted to revive the peace process because continued insurgency could jeopardize its developmental strategy of opening to world markets and attracting foreign investment. Ending the communist insurgency, weak though it had become, may be another sign of internal stability reassuring to investors. For its part, the NDF could hardly afford to ignore the peace process since it provided a forum to voice its alternative agenda and to strengthen its claims for international recognition of belligerency status. At home, however, the NDF, in the face of internal splits and combat losses, still reaffirmed its strategy of protracted people's war. Armando Liwanag, chair of the CPP Central Committee, argued, "The peace negotiations are but one more form of legal struggle that is subordinate to the revolutionary armed struggle."

EXTERNAL SECURITY   China and the projection of Chinese power into the South China Sea continue to dominate Philippine external security concerns. In Filipino eyes, the country's territorial and maritime security is tightly linked to its conflict with China over some islands in the South China Sea and its strategic location in East Asia. Thus management of the Chinese relationship is a vitally important challenge facing the Philippine government.

In 1995, the Chinese occupation of the Panganiban Reef (Mischief Reef) was a wake-up call for the Philippines. In 1996, China ratified the United Nations Convention on the Law of the Sea (UNCLOS) and declared its intention to abide by it in the South China Sea. In addition, President Jiang Zemin in November 1996 reassured the Philippines of China's peaceful intentions and friendliness. These Chinese pledges resulted in renewed optimism in the region that the disputes could be resolved peacefully. Then in April 1997, China sent two armed frigates to the Spratlys areas claimed by the Philippines and Vietnam. The Filipinos were again angered. However, because of their inferior military capability, they could not respond in kind. Hence, the Philippines urged China to abide by the 1992 Manila Declaration on the South China Sea and UNCLOS. Furthermore, the Department of Foreign Affairs reiterated the earlier proposal of Ramos calling for demilitarization of the area and joint development of its resources. Ramos had advanced the idea of "placing the disputed islands under the stewardship of the claimant country closest to it geographically, on the understanding that the stewardship accommodates the other claimants' needs for shelter, anchorage, and other peaceful pursuits."

The Philippine government views the Association of Southeast Asian Nations (ASEAN), the ASEAN Regional Forum (ARF), the United States, and Japan as significant in light of the challenges it faces in its relations with China. ASEAN, for example, magnifies the diplomatic power of the Southeast Asian claimants to stand up against China and provides a venue for bringing the discussion of the South China Sea claims to the multilateral level. In particular, the Philippines has used the ASEAN-China Senior Officials Meeting, the ASEAN-7 plus 1 Post-Ministerial Conferences,* and the Informal Workshop on Managing Potential Conflicts in the South China Sea sponsored by Indonesia to push its proposals for resolution of the territorial dispute with China. ARF also proved to be an important multilateral foreign policy tool for the Philippines. During the 1996 ARF Senior Officials Meeting in Yogyakarta, the Philippines successfully pushed for an extensive discussion of the South China Sea with the full participation of China.

The Philippine elite recognizes that Japan and the United States can exert greater influence on China. Thus, the government supports the stabilizing role of the U.S. presence in the region. For the Philippines, the September 1997 Guidelines for U.S.-Japan Defense Cooperation were welcome as underlining and supporting a continuing U.S. commitment to Asia Pacific security. Similarly, the call in January 1997 by Japan's Prime Minister Hashimoto Ryutaro for a deeper relationship with ASEAN was positively received in the Philippines. According to Hashimoto, the ASEAN-Japan relationship could be strengthened through subregional cooperation to settle disputes and conflicts and through regionwide political dialogue to enhance mutual assurance. Philippine authorities agreed, but cautioned that Japan's regional role must be developed within the framework of the U.S.-Japan Security Treaty and multilateral arrangements such as ARF.

Other external issues affecting domestic security are of concern to the Philippines. These include the agenda of "new" security issues, such as transnational crime and drug trafficking. The Philippines is said to be one of the connecting points for drug traffickers in East Asia. To deal with this matter more effectively, the Philippine government

---

* ASEAN-7 plus 1 refers to the then seven members of ASEAN plus China.

forged a cooperation agreement with Myanmar to prevent trafficking of drugs and other related substances. It has also joined and sponsored a meeting of INTERPOL, a worldwide network for exchanging information on transnational crimes.

Defense Policy and Issues

DEFENSE OBJECTIVES AND PRIORITIES   National security, according to the Ramos administration, is based on the country's economic strength, political unity, and social cohesion. This implies that national security is basically rooted in the domestic condition. The defense establishment therefore continued to function according to these priorities even though there is growing pressure to focus more on external defense. Military personnel are involved in national development projects, assist in the peace process and in the conduct of the local elections, and spearhead disaster preparedness and rescue operations, rehabilitation, and relief assistance. The military engagement in internal security, however, is limited to areas where insurgency is strong. The primary responsibility for internal peace and order has been entrusted to the Philippine National Police (PNP), but the PNP has yet to acquire the training and fighting capability needed for effective counter-insurgency warfare.

Also, because of the increasing need for self-reliance, the government vigorously moved to strengthen the external defense role of the military. Particularly for 1997, officer education placed more emphasis on understanding security concerns of other countries and the potential for a more active Philippine role in regional confidence-building measures. For instance, foreign visits of Philippine military personnel and students diversified to include not only the United States but also Australia, China, Japan, and other ASEAN countries. The military has increased its participation in intergovernmental consultations (such as ARF) and track two diplomacy (such as meetings of the Council for Security Cooperation in Asia Pacific). New defense cooperation agreements were forged with Australia, France, Malaysia, and the United Kingdom. Moreover, the AFP held 14 joint exercises with the U.S. and ASEAN militaries with the objective of testing their defense capabilities and interoperability. In addition, the three services conducted joint training exercises, including air-to-ground, air-amphibious, rapid deployment, and naval-to-air exercises.

MILITARY MODERNIZATION PROGRAM One key area of the AFP modernization program is the streamlining of the military organization. It is expected that the modernization program would result in a total reduction of 31,686 personnel (see table 1). Because of the decreasing need for ground combat forces, the army will have the greatest reduction, 20,781 personnel over a 10-year period. Decreases will be much smaller for the navy and air force. In 1996, restructuring was already initiated, including the deactivation of the Office of Chief Women Auxiliary Corps, the consolidation of seven naval districts into four, and the elimination of 37 paramilitary companies with a

Table 1. Modernization Program for the Armed Forces of the Philippines

Branch of Service	1995	Phase I (1996–2000)	Phase II (2001–2005)	Total Reduction
GHQ	12,356	9,971	7,000	5,355
Air Force	18,223	16,803	16,118	1,237
Navy	25,814	25,313	24,665	1,227
Army	70,293	65,168	53,625	20,781
Total	126,686	107,876	95,000	31,686

SOURCE: Armed Forces of the Philippines, 1997.

strength of 2,232 men. On the other hand, because of the threat of terrorism, the AFP created a Counter-Terrorist Force and upgraded the 505th Search and Rescue Group of the Philippine air force and the Special Operations Command of the Philippine army.

The Congress allocated P50 billion (US$14.2 billion at US$1 = P3.52) for the first phase of the modernization. For the 15 years, the army will get an allocation of P18.4 billion (US$5.2 billion). The air force will receive P59 billion (US$16.8 billion) over 21 years, and the navy will be allocated P70 billion (US$19.9 billion). In 1996, the AFP procurement and upgrading of inventories were minimal. The army acquired an additional 53 SIMBA armored vehicles through coproduction with a British company based in the Subic Port area. The air force procured two F-5 aircraft, and the navy upgraded three coastal patrol interdiction craft, four patrol ships, and two fast attack craft patrol.

In 1997, there were further delays in implementing the modernization effort, largely because of the devaluation of the peso. The secretary of defense said that the Department of National Defense may need to negotiate with the Congress for additional appropriations.

Another major component of the modernization is bases/support system development. In 1996, conversion and relocation of bases and stations began.

Contributions to Regional and Global Security

The Philippine contribution to regional and global peace stemmed primarily from its strengthened domestic condition, which was a result of the success of the peace process with the MNLF, the cease-fire agreement with the MILF, and the country's commitment to democratization. The breakthroughs in the southern Philippines permitted the government to focus more on the problems of development in this area as well as in other parts of the country. Better economic conditions should reduce the sources of dissidence in the future. Meanwhile, the country's democratization and the restoration of economic progress despite the Asian financial crisis demonstrate to other countries that economic development and democratization are compatible.

Given a relatively stable internal system, the Philippines has been able to assume a more active role in international and multilateral diplomacy, thus providing a more substantive contribution to regional and global security.

ENHANCED BILATERAL RELATIONS The Philippine government believes that one way to promote regional and international security is to enhance bilateral relations with neighboring states and other nonregional states. With its ASEAN partners, the Philippines shares the view that an interlocking web of bilateral relations is a necessary step toward building a healthy security community in the absence of a Southeast Asian defense alliance. Joint exercises and border patrols were conducted in June 1996 with ASEAN partners. These included the Philippine-Malaysia Second Coordinated Border Patrol, the Joint Naval Border Patrol with Indonesia, and the AFP and Singapore Armed Forces joint training exercise involving the navy and the air force. A meeting between the armed forces chiefs of staff of Brunei and the Philippines was also held. In addition, former Defense Secretary Renato de Villa visited Vietnam in October 1996. At this time, the two countries agreed to establish a Joint Marine Scientific Research Expedition on the South China Sea. The research expedition was aimed to collect oceanographic data and information on the evolution of the maritime environment.

Ramos paid visits to other ASEAN states. He welcomed the visit of the ousted Cambodian First Prime Minister Prince Norodom Ranariddh to the Philippines, and expressed Philippine support for the elections in Cambodia in 1998. Foreign Affairs Secretary Domingo Siazon headed the ASEAN Standing Committee to negotiate with the Cambodia parties following the July coup by Second Prime Minister Hun Sen. Some, however, criticized the Philippine government and its ASEAN partners for intervening in Cambodia's internal affairs. Siazon, other foreign policy makers, and Philippine foreign policy analysts responded that ASEAN cannot afford to ignore or ostracize Cambodia, as it did with Myanmar in the past.

Philippine bilateral security initiatives extended beyond ASEAN. Joint exercises between the Philippine and U.S. forces continued. To facilitate bilateral military exercises between the two forces, an agreement on the status of forces was being considered. Issues related to criminal jurisdiction remain controversial, and the agreement will undoubtedly face close scrutiny in the Congress.

With China, the Philippines explored areas of common interest and measures for promoting greater transparency and confidence. At the bilateral meeting held on March 13–16, 1996, in Beijing, China and the Philippines decided to establish working groups to discuss and pursue cooperative efforts in relatively noncontroversial issues such as fisheries, environmental protection, and suppression of piracy, smuggling, and drug trafficking. They also agreed to intensify confidence-building through increased military exchanges, dialogue, and visits by military officials. Following this meeting, de Villa visited Beijing and Fu Quanyou, chief of staff of the People's Liberation Army (PLA), came to Manila in September 1996 and PLA Vice-Chief of Staff Xiong Guangkai came in May 1997. The highlight of these exchanges was the state visit of Jiang to Manila in November 1996.

The exchanges between China and the Philippines resulted in the following agreements:
- the opening of an additional consulate general for each side (Guangzhou, Davao);
- the maintenance of the Philippine consulate general in Hong Kong after the handover;
- measures to tap economic complementarities, narrow the trade imbalance, and explore science and technology cooperation;
- enhanced efforts to avoid maritime conflicts;
- the establishment of working groups to explore cooperation

in fisheries, marine environment protection, and confidence-building;
- the exchange of defense and armed forces attachés in Beijing and Manila; and
- the implementation of China's US$3 million military equipment assistance loan.

REGIONAL INITIATIVES   In 1996, the Philippines signed the Treaty on the Southeast Asia Nuclear-Weapon-Free Zone. The treaty prohibits the dumping, disposing, or discharging of radioactive waste and other radioactive materials on land or into the sea or atmosphere within Southeast Asia. Also reflecting the country's concern for the safe use of nuclear energy on a regional basis and the safe shipment of nuclear wastes, Ramos called on East Asians to create an ASIATOM (modeled on the European Atomic Energy Community, or EUROTOM), aimed at consolidating regional attention, consultation, and cooperation on nuclear safety management. This effort was intended to complement the International Atomic Energy Agency. The ASIATOM proposal was reiterated by the Philippines in the March 1997 ARF inter-sessional group (ISG) meeting, which it cochaired with China.

A greater regional security role awaits the Philippines in 1998. As the incoming chair of ARF, the Philippines plans to concentrate on maritime cooperation and a greater role for the military and defense officials in the ARF process. Rodolfo Severino, former undersecretary for plans and policy of the Department of Foreign Affairs, was elected secretary-general of ASEAN.

GLOBAL COMMITMENTS   Along with Australia, Cambodia, Canada, and New Zealand, the Philippine government spearheaded the fight for a total global ban of antipersonnel land mines. It made the land mine issue a priority during the March 1997 ARF ISG meeting as well as the fourth ARF Senior Officials Meeting in Malaysia in May. Through the cooperation of the International Committee of the Red Cross, the Philippine government hosted the Asian Regional Seminar on Land Mines. The Manila conference was significant as the first examination by defense analysts of the use of land mines in Asia. This conference specifically called for government support for negotiations on a treaty to prohibit antipersonnel land mines to be concluded by the end of 1997; rapid adoption of a regional agreement to prohibit remotely delivered antipersonnel land mines to prevent an escalation of mine warfare and higher levels of civilian casualties; and greater regional cooperation in mine clearance and victim assistance.

In spite of its limited resources, the Philippines remained committed to the UN peacekeeping operations. This commitment was made evident by the country's promptly meeting financial obligations to the United Nations and sending police and military contingents to peacekeeping operations. In 1996, the Philippines, upon the request of the United Nations, extended the deployment of 20 personnel forming the second RP-Guard Contingent to Iraq.

Since 1996, the Philippine government has supported moves to reform the UN Security Council. Specifically, it favored the expansion of membership of the Security Council, both permanent and nonpermanent, provided there is an equitable representation of the UN members. In this light, the Philippine government endorsed the bids of Japan and Germany for permanent Security Council positions.

The Philippines declared support for other UN reforms, including more transparency in the working methods of the Security Council; enhanced cooperation between it and the General Assembly; democratization of Security Council decision-making processes, such as limitation of the veto power; and limitation of the "cascade effect" of permanent membership, that is, the unwritten privileges of membership beyond those provided for in the Charter.

12 Russia

THE SECURITY ENVIRONMENT

INTERNAL SECURITY Russia's political condition is characterized by growing stability at the national level but some reemergence of rivalries previously held in check in the face of a communist challenge. Boris Yeltsin, having bested Gennadi Zyuganov in the 1996 polls and overcome his health problems, emerged in the spring of 1997 as a vigorous leader. He reshuffled the government, leaving Prime Minister Viktor Chernomyrdin in place but giving broad powers to the two younger first deputy prime ministers, Anatoly Chubais and Boris Nemtsov. The annual presidential message in March 1997 outlined an impressive reform package, including a new tax code and pension and land reforms.

The government's relations with the opposition, whose stronghold is the lower house of parliament (State Duma), resemble a controlled conflict, with both sides having an important stake in preserving a modicum of political stability. Compromise has prevailed in recent crises. The next parliamentary election is scheduled for late 1999, followed by the presidential election in mid-2000.

Meanwhile, the economy showed signs of improvement. After nine straight years of negative growth (gross national product has fallen 43 percent since 1990), the Russian economy stabilized in 1997, offering prospects for the start of real growth in 1998. Growth, however, may be only 1 percent to 2 percent, owing to the spillover effects of the Asian financial crisis.

Russia continues to face an ideological vacuum created by the collapse of communism. Influential groups still support imperialism, the raison d'être of the Russian state, but imperialism is considered too costly by the increasingly pragmatic leadership and fails to resonate with a citizenry that is progressively more independent of the state. Ethnic Russian nationalism lacks broad support among both the elites and the bulk of the Russian people. The government's policy to build a citizenship-based Russian nation has met with some opposition in the non-Russian republics of the Federation, who fear assimilation. Yeltsin's 1996 decree on developing a new ideology of enlightened patriotism is unlikely to provide even a surrogate ideology.

Tensions continue in relations between Moscow and the increasingly independent regions. The Kremlin has sought to conform regional legislation to the federal Constitution, and has used selective pressures against regional leaders in disfavor. However, as the case of Evgenii Nazdratenko, the governor of Primorie, shows, unseating regional leaders is not easy. Since 1996, the majority of regional governors have a direct popular mandate, potentially amounting to a revolution in Russian governance. The role of regional elites is likely to grow, with the upper chamber of parliament, the Council of the Federation, assuming more political prominence.

The Northern Caucasus continues to be Russia's main domestic security concern. The security situation in Chechnya is generally calm, though still tense. The end of the war, following the humiliating defeat of Russian forces in Grozny, marked a watershed in Russian policies in the Caucasus. Military force has been greatly downgraded as a political instrument. After the hostilities stopped in late August 1996, all remaining Russian forces were withdrawn from the breakaway republic by January 1997. In May 1997, Yeltsin and Chechen President Aslan Maskhadov signed a treaty that effectively recognized the Maskhadov government but stopped short of recognizing Chechnya's independence. Under the August 1996 Khasavyurt peace agreements, this must be resolved before 2001.

Tensions increased in some other parts of the Caucasus. In August 1997, relations worsened between the small republics of North Ossetia-Alania and Ingushetia. The relative stability of Dagestan, peopled by some 30 ethnic groups, is also threatened. Thus, despite the clear tilt toward use of economic levers, Moscow's Caucasus policies have failed so far to produce tangible results.

In 1996, the Russian government adopted yet another regional development program for Eastern Siberia and the Far East emphasizing private Russian and foreign investment to develop the region's natural resources. Sakhalin and Irkutsk energy projects are key to the program. Meanwhile, economic problems and social dislocations continue to plague the relatively backward Far East. Primorie has emerged as one of the main areas of popular discontent, aggravated by political infighting and confrontation with the central government.

EXTERNAL SECURITY   The Russian leadership believes that near-term external dangers to national security are minimal. Chernomyrdin stated in December 1997 that Russia does not expect a major military threat to emerge during the next 10 years. Despite unhappiness with the enlargement of the North Atlantic Treaty Organization (NATO), and the growing competition in the Caspian Sea basin, Russia's vital interests do not clash with those of the major Western countries. Arms control agreements make any surprise attack highly unlikely. Finally, Russia has a formidable nuclear deterrent.

In Asia, some influential Russian analysts do not rule out a serious rise of tensions with China over Transbaikal or Primorie, or competition in Central Asia or Mongolia. They believe this scenario poses the greatest longer-term danger to Russia's national security. Some argue that Russian forces require a transcontinental power projection capability to deter and rebuff a hypothetical Chinese threat. However, there is no agreement within the Russian foreign policy and defense establishment about the longer-range implications of the rise of China, whose GNP may potentially reach 10 times or more that of Russia.

Other dangers may rise, mainly in the South, due to instability prevailing along Russia's southern periphery. Russia is already deeply engaged in order-maintenance in the ethnically complex and conflict-ridden areas once within the Soviet Union. The Commonwealth of Independent States (CIS), a loose association of 12 post-Soviet states, which Moscow hoped could become a Russia-led integrated space giving credence to Russia's claim as an international "pole" of power, has been in disarray since its foundation in December 1991. The CIS summit meeting in Chisinau, Moldova, in October 1997 only confirmed the drifting apart of the former Soviet republics.

Military cooperation within the CIS is limited to a Joint Air Defense system formally including Armenia, Belarus, Georgia, Kazakhstan, Kyrgyzstan, Russia, Tajikistan, Turkmenistan, Ukraine, and Uzbekistan. Joint protection of borders with non-CIS states has linked Russia to Armenia, Belarus, Georgia, Kazakhstan, Kyrgyzstan, and

Tajikistan. Of these, Russia continues to maintain border troops in the two Central Asian and two Transcaucasian states. Although Russia has peacekeeping operations under the CIS mandate in Tajikistan and Abkhazia (since 1993 and 1994, respectively), in October 1997 all countries except Tajikistan rejected Moscow's proposal to create a CIS committee on peacekeeping empowered to deal with violent conflicts and dispatch forces.

Developments in several key bilateral relationships, however, have improved Russia's security environment. In May 1997, after five years of tensions and uncertainty, and against the advice of many of his associates, Yeltsin moved decisively to improve relations with Ukraine. Steps included a political treaty recognizing Ukraine's independence within its present borders and the division of the Black Sea Fleet. Russia muted its criticism of the Sea Breeze '97 Partners for Peace naval exercise off the Crimea, refrained from criticizing the charter on distinct partnership between Ukraine and NATO, and conducted its first-ever joint naval exercise with Ukraine in October 1997.

Russia has so far resisted a temptation to merge with Belarus, despite that country's desire to do so. Financial and economic considerations, as well as concern about the lack of political freedoms in that country, made the Russian government abstain from too close a union.

Moscow continues to seek to build a solid relationship with Kazakhstan. A major political treaty is being prepared, although the relationship still has many points of tension. In the military sphere, Russia and Kazakhstan conducted their first joint command post exercise, Redoubt-97, on the Volga in mid-1997.

NATO enlargement, a burr in Russia's relations with the West since 1993, suddenly lost its prominence as a political issue in Moscow following the signing in Paris in May 1997 of the Founding Act of Mutual Relations, Cooperation and Security between the Russian Federation and NATO. Disagreements remain, but there is a prospect of building a special relationship between Russia and the alliance. In the second half of 1997, several meetings were held of the NATO-Russia Permanent Joint Council (PJC), which is slowly emerging as a mechanism for consultation and interaction. The PJC decided to concentrate on peacekeeping, the Russian Individual Partnership Program under the Partners for Peace, and nuclear weapons-related cooperation. Russia's attempts to discuss the issue of NATO infrastructure in the new member states, however, were unsuccessful. Although some in the

Russian elite continue to be concerned over NATO's increased involvement with the newly independent states of the former USSR, the Russian government is taking a cooperative attitude.

Having largely overcome the crisis over NATO enlargement, the Russian government has concentrated on "the Denver agenda" (after "the Summit of Eight" midyear Denver meeting), that is, a set of economic and financial issues. These, for the first time, have replaced geopolitics as Russia's "high politics."

Defense Policies and Issues

MILITARY REFORM   Since 1991, the Russian defense establishment has been allowed to deteriorate to a state of deep crisis. The combination of a sharp fall of morale and the loosening of security around weapons arsenals, including the nuclear ones, is fraught with potentially disastrous consequences. However, Yeltsin's victory at the polls, the humiliating military defeat in Chechnya, and the desperate state of the Russian armed forces have at last created the conditions for the start of military reform, long advertised but never attempted in earnest. The reform has begun with a practical agenda even before the completion of doctrinal review, initiated with the adoption in 1993 of Russia's new military doctrine.

After much controversy, the president officially approved reform plans in July 1997. Priorities include the continued development of the strategic nuclear deterrent, which is viewed as the principal guarantor of Russia's national security under conditions of conventional weakness; creation of a core of fully capable and well-equipped units and formations, deployed to prevent and neutralize conflicts along Russia's periphery; and qualitative improvement of the officer corps. Progressive professionalization of the armed forces is at the heart of the reform effort and is consonant with the logic of market-driven reforms for the country as a whole. However, Yeltsin's 1996 decree that an all-voluntary force should end the need for conscription by the year 2000 is not considered credible.

MANPOWER AND RESTRUCTURING   One aspect of reform is to optimize force structure. Decisions have been made on which units and formations will remain in the future Russian Armed Forces, and which will be phased out. All military districts—whose number shall be reduced from eight to six—will be given the authority of joint interagency operational-strategic commands, responsible for all military forces in their area of responsibility.

The Strategic Rocket Forces (SRF), the Military Space Forces, and the Missile Defense Forces were merged under the SRF even ahead of the January 1998 deadline. The new service will number 160,000 officers and personnel and 46,000 civilians, an overall reduction of 85,000. The Ground Forces Headquarters will be downgraded and the position of the commander-in-chief of the Ground Forces abolished.

By January 1, 1999, the Air Defense Forces will be integrated within the new air force, thus cutting the number of armed services from five to four. By 2005, Russia should adopt the classical tri-service structure.

The navy, which has been halved since 1991, will keep its four-fleet structure (in the Arctic and Pacific oceans, the Black and Baltic seas, plus the Caspian flotilla), but the number of ships will be drastically reduced and the missions much more modest. In the Pacific, the Russian navy will continue to be based mainly in Primorie and Kamchatka. The reduction of the Pacific Fleet will be carried out in phases, in 1997–98 and 1999–2001. Already the Pacific Fleet has only a third the number of major surface combatants as Japan, and about the same number of torpedo-armed submarines.

Overall, the armed forces military personnel will be reduced to 1,200,000 by 1999. There are projections of an even sharper reduction, to below one million, beyond the year 2000. Officials deny reports of an even more massive downsizing to 650,000, but this is no longer unthinkable. Russia's population, now 147 million, is decreasing. The pool of conscripts is 1.7 million, of which some 400,000 are called up each year. Because of exemptions and competition with other security agencies, some 40 percent of private positions remain unfilled.

DEFENSE BUDGET   Russia's share in the world's gross domestic product has dropped to about 2 percent, and the country is home to about 2.5 percent of the world's population. Nevertheless, Russia accounts for about 4 percent of world defense expenditures and 6 percent of military personnel. This burden, a heritage of the Soviet era, is virtually impossible to carry much longer.

Tremendous budget constraints create pressures for reform but also inhibit implementation. In the short run, downsizing and a drastic reduction of military arsenals are costlier than retention of the superfluous assets. However, small steps are being made. For the first time, the fiscal year 1997 budget included an item for force reduction, and this is likely to be continued in the fiscal 1998 budget. Russia's defense expenditures continue to decrease. From 5.6 percent of GDP in 1994, they rose to 6.38 percent in 1995 due to the Chechen war, but then fell again. In 1997, Russia spent 3.26 percent of GDP on defense. This level is likely to increase only slightly and remain between 3.4 percent and 3.9 percent until the year 2000.

Military reform envisages restructuring the budget and improving accountability. Combat training is a top priority, and reformers want to triple procurement by 2001 and increase it another 1.5 times by 2005. Priorities include nuclear weapons, their delivery systems, precision-guided munitions, information warfare, and C3I systems. Overall, the share of research and development and procurement should rise to 40 percent of the defense budget by 2005.

The social cost of reform will be heavy. The government has finally moved to pay wage arrears to the military, in most cases going back three or more months, thus defusing a potentially dangerous situation. There are plans to double military pay by 2001, and then to raise it 2.5 times again by 2005.

Rehabilitation of retirees is an especially acute issue. More than 170,000 officers and warrant officers will have been retired by 2000. They want not only compensation for early retirement but also help with housing. In 1997, 100,000 service personnel and 150,000 retired officers had no proper housing.

OTHER FORCES   Military reform should cover not only the Ministry of Defense but also other military-related agencies. Over a dozen ministries and agencies have their own armed formations, including the Interior Troops of the Ministry of Internal Affairs (260,000), the Federal Border Service (230,000), the Railroad Troops (80,000), and the Emergency Ministry Troops (70,000). Another 100,000 are in the Construction Troops. In September 1997, a State Military Inspectorate was established under the president to oversee military reform in all government agencies. Since then, the Ministry of Internal Affairs has been more and the Border Service somewhat less eager to synchronize their reform agendas with the Ministry of Defense. Having overcome the General Staff's pressure to integrate into a Ministry of Defense–led structure, the Border Troops are shedding their heavy equipment and are being gradually transformed into paramilitary border guards. The Interior Troops, too, have apparently passed the peak of their numerical growth, and in the aftermath of Chechnya they are de-emphasizing their combat role.

OPPOSITION TO REFORM   General Lev Rokhlin, a Chechen war hero and chair of the Duma Defense Committee, is the most vigorous opponent of reform. In September 1997, he founded a movement to defend the army and the defense science and military industry, which is broadly supported by the Communist Party of the Russian Federation, the National Republican Party of Russia, and other patriotic groups. Rokhlin claims that the government is creating a "police state" by deliberately weakening the armed forces through the reform program and building up "other troops." Despite being well organized, the movement appears to stand no chance to "peacefully oust the government"—its proclaimed aim—unless the government is fatally weakened by a political crisis or reverts to the practice of failing to pay the military for months on end.

DEFENSE INDUSTRY   Since 1990, Russia's defense procurements have been drastically reduced. In 1995, Russia spent the equivalent of US$8 billion on arms and equipment and US$5 billion on research and development. Conversion has been largely a failure, although some companies, especially in the aerospace industry, have managed to adapt to the market-driven environment. Unless more enterprises follow suit, the bulk of the defense industry will disappear. The reform agenda for Russia's defense industry focuses on enhancing its high-tech and dual-technology potential. However, the start of massive modernization of the forces' arsenals has been delayed to 2005, to be completed by 2025. Where not involved in export projects, the defense industry is in a state of near desperation.

ARMS SALES   Russian arms deliveries continue to increase. In 1997, sales amounted to US$7 billion to US$10 billion. Three-quarters of arms exports go to just three countries: China, India, and Iran. China alone buys twice as many weapons as the Russian Ministry of Defense itself. In 1992–93, Russia sold China Su-27 fighter-interceptor aircraft and S-300 PMU air defense systems. In 1994, China agreed to buy more S-300 and four submarines. In 1995, Russia sold another 22 Su-27s and agreed to sell technology for producing the Su-27 SK in China, allowing China to produce 15 aircraft a year. Other agreements with China cover future sales of the Tor-M1 short-range air defense system, several Sovremennyy-class destroyers, and Ka-28 and Ka-27 naval helicopters.

The arming of China in parallel with Russian military reductions in Asia and the overall weakening of Russia's Far Eastern provinces is controversial. Some elites support expanded sales on economic grounds, and others urge caution. This split is a vivid example of the Russian elite's continued inability to agree on the national interest.

Contributions to Regional and Global Security

ASIA PACIFIC ROLE   Asia Pacific is emerging as an autonomous dimension of Russia's foreign and security policies. Moscow is adjusting its recent tilt toward Beijing in favor of more engagement with Tokyo. It is not inconceivable that a triangular Sino-Russo-Japanese relationship could emerge within a broader quadrangle including the United States.

Relations with China, officially called a strategic (i.e., long-term) partnership, remain extremely important. In 1997, Yeltsin and President Jiang Zemin exchanged official visits, praising the concept of a multipolar world but cutting short talk of an incipient alliance. China sympathizes with the Russian position on NATO enlargement, and Russia sides with China on Taiwan, Tibet, and Xinkiang.

Following the 1996 border accord between China, Russia, Kazakhstan, Kyrgyzstan, and Tajikistan, the five signed an agreement in April 1997 on confidence-building measures along the 4,200-kilometer border. These border agreements and confidence-building measures are especially important. The former Soviet-Chinese border is now properly demarcated, with remaining differences confined to three islands near Khabarovsk and on the Argun River. The forces deployed within a 100-kilometer-wide strip running along both sides of the border will be reduced, and a series of confidence-building measures has been agreed on.

The improvements in Russia's relationship with Japan intensified after a July speech by Prime Minister Hashimoto Ryutaro calling for "engaging" Russia. In November 1997, the first-ever informal "no neckties" summit between the two countries' leaders was held in Krasnoyarsk. In a surprise move, they agreed to set a year 2000 deadline for signing a peace treaty between the two countries. An action plan emphasized economic cooperation. The two countries plan more military exchanges and may conduct a military exercise. Even before the Krasnoyarsk summit, in 1996–97, the first exchange of visits of defense ministers occurred, and a Russian naval ship entered Tokyo Bay for the first time this century. In a dramatic departure from Soviet statements, Defense Minister Igo Nikolayevich Rodionov during his May 1997 visit to Japan called the U.S.-Japan Security Treaty a stabilizing factor in Northeast Asia. Both Moscow and Tokyo seek to de-emphasize the territorial issue, which they are unable to solve in the immediate future.

Russia has had both successes and disappointments in its efforts to strengthen its role in multilateral Asia Pacific diplomacy. In 1996, it became a full participant of the ASEAN Regional Forum, and in November 1997 the member economies of Asia-Pacific Economic Cooperation agreed that Russia could join that important forum, probably in 1998. However, Russia remains unhappy about its exclusion from the Four-Party Talks on Korea. Since Russia's main Korean links are now with the South, some call for restoring a degree of influence in the North. Russian officials believe that a united Korea could be a valuable regional partner for Moscow.

ROLE IN EUROPE   Russia has tried to solidify its relations with the major European countries. It was announced that it will hold annual trilateral summit meetings with France and Germany, the first of which is planned for April 1998 in the Russian city of Yekaterinburg, straddling the Europe-Asia boundary. Policies also have become more pragmatic with regard to the Baltic States. Although sensitive to possible Baltic membership in NATO, Russia is showing flexibility on bilateral issues. In October 1997, Russia signed a border treaty with Lithuania, and offered all three Baltic states unilateral security guarantees, which were predictably rejected. Moscow continued in December with plans to cut its conventional forces in Northwestern Russia by 40 percent.

PEACEKEEPING   Russia's most significant contributions to international security involve other republics formed from the Soviet Union. In the summer of 1997, together with the United Nations and Iran, Russia brokered a peace accord in troubled Tajikistan, ending a five-year-old civil war. The agreement appears to be holding. Russia continues to keep a sizable peacekeeping force in the country as well as 17,000 Russian-led but locally conscripted border troops.

In Transcaucasus, Russian reluctance to expand its mandate to ensure the safe return of Georgian refugees to Abkhazia led to a permanent state of tension between Moscow and Tbilisi. In contrast, Russia's peacekeeping mission in South Ossetia remains largely noncontroversial. Russia has joined the United States and France, two other prominent members of the Minsk group on Nagorno-Karabakh, in an effort to bring about a peaceful settlement of this dispute. The cease-fire between Armenia and Azerbaijan, first negotiated with Russian assistance in May 1994, is holding.

Russian diplomacy has been trying to bring about dispute resolution in Moldova, but it has encountered new problems. The leadership of the breakaway Dnestr republic is obstinate, and Ukraine seeks to become more prominent as a peacemaker, both as a partner and a rival of Russia.

Outside the old Soviet space, the Russian brigade continued its mission in Bosnia-Herzegovina. Military cooperation with NATO forces in that country remains excellent. With the termination of the UN mission in Croatia, Russia withdrew its battalion from Eastern Slavonia.

ARMS CONTROL   With the new emphasis on economic relations with its Group of Eight partners, arms control issues are less prominent in Russia's relations with the West. Russia and the United States signed a protocol on the Strategic Arms Reduction Treaty 2 (START-2) that, in view of Russia's financial and technical difficulties, extends the implementation for the reductions by four years to the end of 2007. Despite these adjustments and the fact of U.S. ratification in January 1996, the Duma has yet to give its consent. Russia and the United States started exploratory talks on a START-3 reducing their respective strategic nuclear arsenals to 2,000–2,500 weapons.

In November 1997, the Duma ratified the Chemical Weapons Convention, reversing an earlier decision. Yeltsin in October 1997 promised Russia's accession to the treaty banning land mines, but it is unclear how and when Russia can start implementing the treaty, if it indeed signs it.

13 Singapore

THE SECURITY ENVIRONMENT

NATIONAL SECURITY PERCEPTIONS   Two key factors underlie and drive Singaporean perceptions of security and stability in Asia Pacific. The first is historical: collective memories of the Japanese occupation of Singapore during World War II; the constitutional separation, by the British at the end of World War II, of Singapore from Malaya; the drive to merge with Malaysia during the struggle for independence; and the final separation from Malaysia in 1965. The second is geo-economic: Singapore's location as the smallest state in Southeast Asia, its lack of resources, and its dependence upon its entrepôt economy for survival. These fundamentals have led Singaporeans and their leaders to, on the one hand, a rather realist perspective of their environment—that ultimately nobody owes Singapore a living—and, on the other hand, the belief that through trade and investments Singapore could help build up economic interdependence for a more secure and stable Asia Pacific.

Applying these perceptions to the overall regional environment and outlook, Singaporeans can envision a variety of future scenarios, each with its own challenges and possible threats to their country. In an "East Asian Renaissance" scenario, Asia Pacific prospers in a "borderless" world built on the foundations of an open international trading system. The Asia-Pacific Economic Cooperation (APEC) forum is instrumental in reducing regional tariffs and barriers to trade and investments. The Chinese economy is the economic powerhouse of the region. Rapid economic growth and urbanization create an expanding middle class with demands for a new range of consumer goods and services. The U.S. economy receives a larger boost from meeting these new demands from Asia than from the North American Free Trade Agreement. The challenge to Singapore in this projection is that its continued prosperity depends on highly trained and technologically oriented workers, who are very mobile and could migrate, leaving Singapore to be manned by its less skilled citizens. Like the Protestant ethic, this vision of the future reinforces the drive to sustain a competitive edge.

In an alternative "meltdown" scenario, made more plausible by the events of late 1997, the East Asian economic miracle disintegrates. The economic fundamentals that the World Bank and the present generation of leaders thought were entrenched crumble. The Japanese economy stagnates or even shrinks, forcing the Japanese to cut imports and increase exports to the United States and European Union (EU) markets. China matches Japan's increasing exports to maintain its market niche. The EU and the United States retaliate with protectionist initiatives, forcing the world into warring trade blocs. U.S. capital shifts from Asia to Latin America and EU capital withdraws to Eastern Europe. The economic glue that holds the Asian economies together melts, and the disruptive forces of ethnicity and nationalism erupt into domestic violence or conflicts between countries. This is a disaster scenario for Singapore, which might initially be sufficiently nimble to survive but in the medium term and long term would be severely affected and have the greatest difficulty formulating an effective response.

While the Asian Renaissance scenario is not without its challenges for Singapore, it is manageable. However, from the perspective of Singapore's leaders it is of critical importance that the meltdown scenario be avoided.

GLOBAL INTERDEPENDENCE AND SECURITY   At the global level, the principal immediate concern is that the East Asian economic miracle not be perceived as a challenge, and certainly not be seen as a threat, to the United States or the European Union. Rather, ways need to be found to ensure that Asia, America, and Europe in the next millennium complement each other economically and perhaps eventually converge. The Singapore government sees the Asia-Europe Meeting as a significant mechanism for building this complementarity between Asia and Europe, while APEC continues to link Asia with the Americas.

MAJOR POWER RELATIONS   Singapore's leaders believe that the triangular relationship between the United States and Japan and China is the pivot around which the future of Asia Pacific will be shaped. Whether Asia Pacific will move toward more open regionalism in trade will depend in large part upon the evolving U.S.-China relationship. To the extent that the United States can accept the contradiction of China's claim for less-developed-country status and demands for recognition as an emergent regional, if not world, power, and to the extent that China can reassure the United States (and the rest of Asia Pacific) that a resurgent China will be a responsible one, then Asia Pacific may move closer toward an Asian Renaissance scenario. China's attitude toward the United States and Japan is shaped in part by the U.S.-Japan security arrangements, which it perceives as a cold war legacy to contain China. A reconciliation of the historical memories of the Chinese and Japanese is necessary if China is to be assured of the intent of the recent enhancement of those security arrangements.

The Singapore government sees the ASEAN Regional Forum (ARF) as a major venue for the negotiation of this triangular relationship as the foundation of a post–cold war security architecture in Asia Pacific. In its four years of existence, ARF has built up a significant level of trust and confidence among its members, so that differences now are more likely to be resolved peacefully without the use of force. The comfort level that has been achieved among members of ARF should now enable the forum to move from its initial phase of confidence building to the next phase of preventive diplomacy. Much of the work exploring how to move ARF into preventive diplomacy and other related security issues is done at the Inter-Sessional Group Meetings and various track two fora such as the Council for Security Cooperation in Asia Pacific (CSCAP) and the ASEAN Institutes for Strategic and International Studies (ASEAN-ISIS).

SOUTHEAST ASIA   Singapore's relations with Malaysia continue to be sensitive because of the close interdependence between the two countries. Memories of the circumstances leading to Singapore's separation from Malaysia and Singaporean perceptions of vulnerability have a strong influence on the relationship. Serious tensions developed between the two nations in 1997 when remarks by Senior Minister Lee Kuan Yew in a Singapore court affidavit against a political opponent seeking refuge in Malaysia were taken in Malaysia as belittling the country.

The currency crisis that hit most Asia Pacific countries in late 1997 is a test case of whether the economic interdependence that has been built up will work and lead to mutual cooperation. Singapore's rapid provision of financial assistance to Thailand and Indonesia within the framework of the International Monetary Fund demonstrated recognition of this growing economic interdependence.

Defense Policies and Issues

REGIONAL DEFENSE DIPLOMACY The Singapore government continues to pursue a security strategy of developing a capability to deter threats and to underpin this deterrence with a diplomatic framework of defense links and alliances. ARF is seen in Singapore as the most promising diplomatic initiative for a new security architecture in Asia Pacific. Singapore joins its partners in the Association of Southeast Asian Nations in believing that ASEAN should remain the core of the forum to which it gave its name. This is based on the view that ASEAN in its 30 years has consolidated and further defined an Asian way to peace—recognizing differences in values, norms, and practices among nations, stressing the search for commonalities and understanding, and progressing in small steps based on consensus—which draws on earlier Asian experiences and therefore may have relevance to a wider Asia Pacific region.

ARF, the earlier Five Power Defense Arrangements, and other multilateral arrangements, such as the Southeast Asia Nuclear-Weapons-Free Zone sponsored by ASEAN and their supporting track two forums (CSCAP, ASEAN-ISIS), are the weft in the fabric of Southeast Asian security, the warp of which are a series of bilateral links and alliances. Some of these bilateral arrangements are post–World War II and cold war legacies, such as Japan's and the Philippines' links with the United States. Others are more recent, in particular Australia's agreement with Indonesia. Singapore's bilateral defense ties extend from its ASEAN neighbors to powers around ASEAN. These ties have enabled Singapore to achieve a deeper understanding and closer rapport with its friends.

The Singapore government believes that this network of bilateral ties has been a stabilizing influence in the region and should continue. The U.S. forward military presence, based on arrangements with Japan and South Korea, is seen as a major stabilizing force in Northeast

Asia, the influence of which extends to Southeast Asia. The major American investments in the region, and the region's reliance on U.S. technology and markets, reinforce the U.S. security interest in the region and the region's acceptance of the U.S. involvement. The Singapore government accordingly supports continuation of the U.S. military presence.

DEFENSE SPENDING AND FORCES   Singapore recognizes that ultimately its credibility as a nation-state in the community of nations is not only the list of friends it can call upon but equally its foreign reserves and its capability to defend itself and to cooperate with others in the defense of the region.

Singapore continues to spend just under 4 percent of its gross domestic product on defense. In 1997, it budgeted S$6.12 billion (US$3.7 billion at S$1 = US$0.60), or 4.17 percent of its GDP, for defense. This is lower than the previous year's 4.23 percent. Of this, S$5.70 billion (US$3.42 billion), or 93.2 percent of the amount budgeted, is for operating expenditure and the balance of S$418 million (US$250 million), or 6.8 percent, is for development expenditure. Operating expenditures include payment of salaries and allowances of full-time national service personnel and operationally ready national service personnel, maintenance of camps, and purchase of military equipment. The development expenditure is primarily for development of new camps and renovation of old camps.

This expenditure enables Singapore to maintain an army of three combined arms divisions and two People's Defense Force commands; an air force with two squadrons of F-5 Tigers, three squadrons of A4-SU Super Skyhawks, and a squadron each of Hawker Hunters/RF 5 and F-16 Fighting Falcons; and a navy comprising two flotillas of missile corvettes and missile gunboats supported by a Coastal Command and a Logistics Command.

An important part of Singapore's defense strategy is modernization. This includes the recent upgrading of its inventory of aging AMX-13 tanks and the introduction of a new home-designed infantry fighting vehicle to meet the shortfall of M113s in the Singapore Armed Forces (SAF) order of battle. The decision to design and produce a new infantry fighting vehicle was based on the desire to provide the SAF with a platform that matches more closely its operational needs. In 1995, the Singapore navy acquired a decommissioned Royal Swedish Navy Sjoormen-class submarine in order to evaluate the need and feasibility of developing a submarine capability. Subsequently, Sweden offered and Singapore purchased three more decommissioned Sjoormen-class submarines. Perhaps reflecting its awareness of the sensitivities of neighboring states, the Singapore government argued that this was an opportunity buy and did not reflect a final decision to develop an operational submarine capability.

The real challenge for the SAF, however, is not the upgrading and improvement of its hardware, but rather the recruitment and retention of skilled manpower to operate its hardware. In a tight labor market, the SAF has had some difficulty in recruiting and retaining skilled personnel. The Ministry of Defense has, therefore, with the advice of an international human resource consultant, been reviewing its remuneration schemes and plans in 1998 to restructure its remuneration packages to make continued service more attractive for its regular officers. Officers now generally retire at the age of 50 or earlier, compared to their civilian counterparts who work to 60 or more years of age. Persuading some of the best and brightest from each generation of Singaporeans to take on full-time careers in the SAF is a growing problem.

Contributions to Regional and Global Security

Singapore's main contribution to regional and global security is through its strategy of defense diplomacy. The bedrock of its defense diplomacy is an expanding series of bilateral and multilateral military exercises with its ASEAN neighbors, its Five Power Defense Arrangements partners, and the United States. Over the years, annual bilateral navy, air force, and army exercises with Brunei, Indonesia, Malaysia, the Philippines, and Thailand within ASEAN, and with Australia, the United Kingdom, and the United States have grown in scale and complexity.

In 1996 and 1997, Singapore established new bilateral ties, principally with South Africa, France, and Sweden. A major focus of these new agreements is on joint research and development in defense technology. Singapore's Ministry of Defense has also established new forums with its Malaysian and Indonesian counterparts to discuss bilateral security and defense policy issues and regional security developments.

The SAF continues to be active in UN peacekeeping operations. It participated in earlier UN peacekeeping operations in Angola and Cambodia. It now sends a senior officer and supporting staff to the UN Iraq-Kuwait Observation Mission, and medical support staff to the UN peacekeeping mission in Guatemala. Singapore is preparing to join 62 other countries in signing an agreement with the United Nations to formalize its commitment to the UN Standby Arrangements System for peacekeeping operations.

Singapore also cochairs with the United States the ARF intersessional group on air-sea search and rescue. Its CSCAP National Committee in May 1997 hosted the first ever General Meeting of CSCAP. In September 1997, the Institute of Defense and Strategic Studies joined the International Institute for Strategic Studies in London in organizing an ARF track two conference on preventive diplomacy.

14 Thailand

The Security Environment

DOMESTIC DEVELOPMENTS   When Prime Minister Chavalit Yongchaiyudh, a former army commander-in-chief and supreme commander of the armed forces, assumed office on November 25, 1996, little did he know that he was to face Thailand's most daunting political and economic crisis in decades. Politically, a draft Constitution promised unprecedented political reform but was also a source of tremendous controversy. At the same time, Thailand's weakened economy was pitched into a full-blown economic crisis by midyear.

Mainly because of the mounting economic turmoil, Chavalit was forced to resign on November 6, 1997. He was soon replaced by Chuan Leekpai, who also assumed Chavalit's post as defense minister, the second person in Thai political history without any military background to hold this position. (The first person was Prime Minister Seni Pramoj, who held the post for less than a month in 1975.) Despite the fragility of Chuan's coalition, he moved quickly to consolidate his position and to restore domestic and foreign confidence in Thailand as well as to create a positive security environment.

The new Constitution, the 16th since 1932, came into effect on September 27. As the first Constitution to be drafted by a directly elected assembly, it featured democratic values and principles such as popular participation, civil and human rights, government effectiveness, transparency, and accountability. Its adoption was not smooth. In the end, the prime minister and some leading members of the government parties had to be coaxed by leaders of the military and the business community to support the draft Constitution for the sake of national unity and social harmony. For most Thais, the new Constitution was seen not only as necessary for Thai politics and society at this historical juncture but also as an important framework through which the economic reform and revitalization could be achieved.

THE ECONOMIC CRISIS   After almost a decade of unprecedented economic growth, the first warning signs of slowdown came in late 1995. By early 1997, it became increasingly clear that the economic downturn could be serious. The current account deficit was an unsustainable 8 percent of gross national product. Exports were no longer competitive. Direct investments ceased and the stock market was falling. Currency speculators bet against the baht, which was pegged to the U.S. dollar, prompting calls for a swift devaluation to end speculation and regain competitiveness. This was finally done on July 2, but only after the central bank had spent the better part of its reserves in futile attempts to defend the baht.

Its depleted reserve situation forced the Thai government in August 1997 to seek assistance from the International Monetary Fund (IMF) and Asian governments, resulting in a US$17.2 billion bailout program. According to the program, Thailand must strictly follow IMF guidelines. The IMF will closely monitor and evaluate implementation of the program.

The economic situation continued to worsen through the end of the year as the lowered value of the baht and the lack of new capital made it virtually impossible for Thai businesses to pay foreign-denominated loans. The recovery is expected to be prolonged, with as many as two to three million in the country's 25 million work force losing jobs over the coming two years. In a testimony to Thailand's democracy, public protests forced the November change in government, but internal political and social stability may be threatened as the economic dislocations intensify and increasingly affect both skilled and unskilled workers. In the near term, the economic crisis is probably the single biggest threat to Thai well-being, its new democracy, and individual, if not national, security.

INTERNAL SECURITY ISSUES   Aside from the unknown implications of the economic turmoil, the principal internal security issues are Muslim separatists, drug trafficking, and illegal immigration. Despite the government's continued effort to weed out terrorist groups and separatist movements, terrorism remains a serious problem. Thai authorities confirmed that in 1997 at least 50 heavily armed terrorists operate in the South in four Muslim separatist organizations. Thai authorities sought Malaysian cooperation because they believe that the terrorists take refuge across the border. However, Malaysia has consistently insisted that the matter is Thailand's internal affair and that Malaysia cannot interfere. In early 1998, for the first time ever, Malaysia has shown more willingness to cooperate with Thailand on this matter.

In contrast, there was increased cooperation between Thailand, its neighbors, and the UN International Drug Control Program (UNDCP) in countering drug trafficking. According to Thai authorities, there is little that they can do to control narcotic traffic since production is carried out in the country's northern neighbors and Thailand is a consumer. The transit point for shipment to the international market is in Cambodia, and the money laundering, meanwhile, is mostly done in Koh Song, in Myanmar. In July 1997, Thailand signed an agreement on three projects with China, Laos, Myanmar, Vietnam, and the UNDCP to share information and train law enforcement and judicial officials. The military has an important role to play in combating the trafficking of drugs, particularly amphetamine pills, from Cambodia, Laos, and Myanmar.

Illegal migrant workers, particularly from Myanmar, Bangladesh, and elsewhere in South Asia, were another serious problem. According to official Thai estimates, there are at least 800,000 undocumented foreign workers in Thailand, about half from Myanmar. Although the economic downturn has reduced the incentives to immigrate, the inflow has not stopped and continues to pose serious economic and social challenges. There is particular concern that illegal immigration makes the spread of epidemics difficult to contain.

BORDER ISSUES   In 1997, as in most years, Thailand's immediate external security concerns were focused on its long borders. The year, however, proved to be relatively uneventful in this regard. Border differences with Cambodia, Laos, Malaysia, and Myanmar existed, but all incidents were effectively managed, if not resolved. Thailand and its neighbors have apparently reached a new level of maturity in the management of border problems as exemplified by the low level and intensity of border incidents. In particular, the speedy and peaceful settlement of most problems demonstrated the usefulness of the joint border commissions established in the past.

The only serious border concern came in the second half of the year when fighting in Cambodia led to a flood of refugees and a spillover of the fighting. The political turmoil in Cambodia became a full-scale military conflict in June and July 1997, with violent clashes between the troops of First Prime Minister Prince Norodom Ranariddh and Second Prime Minister Hun Sen and the subsequent takeover by Hun Sen forces. As fighting spread to northwestern Cambodia, an estimated 56,000 refugees made their way to the Thai border. For humanitarian reasons, Thai authorities allowed the refugees to shelter in Thai territory until the fighting subsided. In the meantime, warning shots were fired by Thailand's northeastern Suranaree Task Force into Cambodia whenever artillery shells strayed into Thai territory. Stray shells killed one Thai soldier and wounded several others.

Although the fighting has largely abated, the situation remains volatile, and Thai authorities continue to watch for any possible spillover into Thai territory. So far, the Cambodian situation is not regarded as a military security threat, but as a renewal of the political and economic burdens reminiscent of those imposed by the civil war in Cambodia in the 1980s.

Clashes between Myanmar troops and Karen rebels, the Karen National Union, and the massive inflow of Karen refugees into Thailand kept the tension high along the Thai-Myanmar border despite the determination of the two governments to exercise restraint. Yangon authorities often accused Thailand of harboring the Karen rebels and refusing to allow an estimated 90,000 Karen refugees in Thailand to return to Myanmar.

As Thailand and Myanmar have yet to demarcate fully their 2,202-kilometer border, other problems cause occasional disputes. In May and July 1997, for instance, there was a military standoff over an island in the Moei River, opposite Tak Province. Although a crisis was averted, no solution has been reached. Also, after Khun Sa surrendered to Yangon authorities in 1996, Thailand and Myanmar had been locked in a territorial dispute over the drug czar's former stronghold in mountainous terrain straddling their border. No early solution is in sight.

On the 1,830-kilometer Laotian border, Thailand and Laos in May began a survey to further negotiations on demarcation. In the meantime, border incidents between the two countries are still normal occurrences. An October incident involved the abduction of six Thai immigration officers who boarded a Lao cargo vessel allegedly transporting contraband. Maintaining that the vessel was in Laotian waters, Lao authorities refused to return the Thai customs officers and demanded reparation for damages as well as the return of four vessels seized by Thailand. Eventually, the Thai officers were swapped for the Laotian boats and crew.

Another thorny issue is the estimated 13,000 Laotian Hmong who have illegally lived in Thailand for more than 20 years. Thailand has repeatedly requested that Laos take back the Hmongs, but Laos has always refused, arguing that the Hmong are anti-communist and subversive. As in the cases of Cambodia and Myanmar, Thailand's border problems with Laos will remain unsolved as long as comprehensive negotiations cannot be held.

Thailand's border problems with Malaysia in 1997 centered on the separatist movements mentioned above and illegal migrant workers crossing from Thailand into Malaysia. Many illegal immigrants, originating from Myanmar and South Asia, use Thailand's southern provinces as the staging points for travel to Malaysia, other countries, or other parts of Thailand. A Thai-Malaysian dispute over the demarcation of the Kolok River and their maritime boundary in the Gulf of Thailand also remains unsettled.

SOUTHEAST ASIA   Despite border incidents, achievements in relations with Southeast Asian neighbors improved the general climate of regional relations. Indonesia, Malaysia, and Thailand concluded tripartite agreements on overlapping territorial waters; Thailand and Laos signed agreements on border crossing and avoidance of double taxation; the Thai-Myanmar friendship bridge across the Moei River was opened; and Thailand and Vietnam signed an agreement completely demarcating their overlapping maritime boundaries in the Gulf of Thailand.

Beyond its immediate borders, Thailand continued to attach high importance to the security situation in the South China Sea and the Strait of Malacca. This is based on concern that disputes in the region could negatively affect Thai interests rather than a perception of a direct threat to Thai security. As a nonclaimant to territories in the South China Sea, Thailand distanced itself from the disputes while keeping a watchful eye on developments. Thus, it was not surprising that Thailand remained silent when disputes arose between China and Vietnam and China and the Philippines over maritime boundaries. Thailand will likely continue this posture in the foreseeable future.

In 1997, Thailand continued to hold annual joint military exercises with Malaysia and Singapore. However, because of the economic difficulty, it is expected that in the future the exercises will be held less frequently.

THE LARGE POWERS   Thailand's relationships with China on the one hand and with the United States on the other continue to be the main features of the country's security outlook. In 1997, Thailand managed to maintain, if not strengthen, its relationships with these two powers as well as with Japan.

Many analysts describe the relationship with China as "special" because of the close relations between the two countries since diplomatic relations were reestablished in 1975. Chavalit's April 1997 trip to China made him the first East Asian leader to call on the Chinese leadership following the death of Deng Xiaoping. A number of crucial agreements were reached, including a plan to build a road between Bangkok and Yunan Province via Myanmar by the year 2000. China agreed to help Thailand set up a national shipping fleet and acquire oil tankers, and it also offered to sell additional weapons to Thailand at "friendship prices." Although very much interested, the Thais had to refrain from signing any deals because of economic constraints. Later, in August 1997, Thailand became the first country to be offered financial assistance by China within the framework of the IMF.

The friendship and goodwill generated by U.S. President Bill Clinton's visit to Bangkok in November 1996, the first U.S. presidential visit to Thailand in 27 years, continued into 1997. Due to the changing geopolitical and economic environment, however, the relationship between the two countries focused on trade and investment issues. Nevertheless, the two countries maintain close military cooperation. The United States is Thailand's top arms supplier, and Thai military personnel continue to receive scholarships to study in the United States under the International Military Education and Training Program. The United States also proved to be accommodating in agreeing to relax the terms of arms purchase agreements in the face of Thailand's financial hardship. The two countries conduct 40 joint military exercises annually, notably the 16-year-old Cobra Gold naval and marine exercise. Cobra Gold '97 was of special significance since it was the first time that a UN peacekeeping scenario had been employed. Despite these positive features of Thai-U.S. relations, the failure of the United States to provide direct financial assistance to help bail out the Thai economy, aside from its contribution to the IMF program, occasioned severe criticism of U.S. policy among the Thai elites.

Aside from the strategic and security relationships with China and the United States, Thailand's relationship with Japan is an important element in its security outlook. The Thai-Japanese relationship remains focused on economic and trade cooperation. Chavalit visited Tokyo in early October mainly to woo Japanese support for the rehabilitation of the Thai economy. Japan expressed readiness to contribute to Thailand's economic recovery and reforms and was the largest country contributor to the IMF package.

The Thais kept a watchful eye on the new Guidelines for U.S.-Japan Defense Cooperation adopted in September 1997. Unlike in some countries, the Thai military and security establishments were quite receptive to the new guidelines. There was no feeling of hostility or apprehension over a possible expanded security role by Japan's Self-Defense Forces. This probably reflects Thailand's unique lack of bitter wartime experiences with Japan.

Defense Policies and Issues

STRATEGIC POLICY AND OUTLOOK Thailand's strategic outlook and policies reflect a growing sophistication among the leadership of the armed forces about global and regional affairs. While Thailand continues to adhere to its "total defense strategy," under which all available forces make a single combined response to domestic or external threat, the country's defense posture had become less focused on territorial defense and more on the protection of broader national interests. The procurement of *HTMS Chakri Naruebet*, a V(/S)TOL aircraft carrier, reflected this significant change in Thailand's strategic outlook as well as in the assessment of its security role and capabilities. The acquisition demonstrated an interest in power projection, but primarily for the protection of vital economic interests and resources.

In line with this perspective, the Ministry of Defense in April 1997 issued a 222-page report entitled "Vision 2030." This presented the military's perspectives in seven crucial areas: politics, economics, society and culture, defense, science and energy, technology, and quality of life and the environment. It argued that in the long run the military would become increasingly important in securing and protecting national interests, particularly maritime resources. Therefore, Thailand must maintain tactical readiness, while implementing a strong policy of self-reliance. The report also argued against compromising the force structure of the armed forces or the ambitious modernization programs.

According to this report, the United States will likely maintain its regional presence and cooperate militarily with Thailand, but Thailand's strategic importance to the United States has declined. Meanwhile, China's influence will increase in proportion to the decline in Russian power. Under these circumstances, the report recommended that Thailand should promote closer relations with China and look to China to replace obsolete weaponry.

The Defense Ministry report regarded efforts to settle border disputes with Cambodia and Laos as of utmost importance. It also recommended that Thailand help bring Myanmar into the Association of Southeast Asian Nations (ASEAN) to reduce the current border conflicts. The report speculated that Myanmar would continue to strengthen its China ties. Without defining the term, the report argued that Thailand's number one "competitor" now and in the future is Malaysia and that Vietnam could emerge as another "competitor."

In October, the National Security Council (NSC), an intelligence bureau attached to the prime minister's office, issued new policy guidelines for the years 1998–2001. These focused on seven priority areas: domestic politics, the economy, socio-psychological issues, science and technology, energy and the environment, national defense, and foreign policy. The policy guidelines called for a new breed of leadership with the thinking and management skills capable of harnessing domestic strengths and contending with powerful regional and global forces.

The guidelines identified three sets of security threats in the years ahead: those arising from global changes, from unequal domestic economic and social development, and from the economic turbulence. Other external factors such as international economic competition, terrorism, drug trafficking, illicit arms trade, organized crime and money laundering, illegal migrant workers, and disinformation schemes to tarnish the country's image were also seen as threats to Thailand's national interests.

The NSC saw an urgent need for improved mechanisms to give early warning to government leaders and help them understand the challenges and options at hand. In order to preserve the nation's natural resources and energy supplies, the policy also called for enhanced military prowess and diplomatic adeptness. To secure and promote the national interests, the guidelines also proposed that linkages with China, Japan, and the United States be enhanced.

DEFENSE BUDGET   Because of the economic crisis, the government was forced to reduce the national budget substantially. Many projects were put on hold, including those of the armed forces. By October, after three cuts since its original cabinet approval in April, the 1998 defense budget stood at around 85 billion baht (US$1.8 billion at US$1 = B48.15). This was approximately 10.5 percent of the total budget and was the third largest budget after those of the Education and Interior ministries. It represented approximately 2.5 percent of the country's gross domestic product and was actually 18 billion baht (US$374 million) less than the 1997 budget of 104 billion baht (US$2.2 billion), a cutback of 17.6 percent. But the economic crisis will probably force another reduction of perhaps 3 billion baht (US$62 million).

MANPOWER, MODERNIZATION, AND PROCUREMENTS   Thailand's force modernization and procurement programs reflect its new force structure policy, formulated in the early 1990s, which aimed for a smaller but more advanced fighting force through rigorous training and modernization of weaponry. The Royal Thai Army, in particular, continued to pursue its troop reduction plan, which saw a reduction of 15 percent of its forces from 1992 to 1996 and anticipates another 10 percent cut by 2001. Modernization justified many grandiose procurement schemes, which were backed by Chavalit to shore up support among his former military colleagues and supporters. Thus in December 1996, his new administration approved the purchase of a satellite system, eight F/A-18 fighter jets equipped with Advanced Medium Range Air-to-Air Missiles (AMRAAM), two submarines, 295 armored vehicles, approximately 40,000 M16-A2 assault rifles and other light weapons, and 200 combat tanks. The economic crisis forced the suspension of most of these acquisitions or the renegotiation of the purchase agreements.

Since the suspension was not retroactive, a spectacular new addition to the Royal Thai Navy came in the form of a V(/S)TOL aircraft carrier at the height of the country's financial troubles. Named the *HTMS Chakri Naruebet* (The Great Chakri Dynasty) and commissioned in August, the Spanish-built carrier was the first in Southeast Asia and cost US$280 million. The ship has a full-load displacement of 11,485 tons and a maximum operational range of 10,000 nautical miles at an average speed of 12 knots. It came equipped with six multi-mission Sikorsky SH-70B Sea Hawk helicopters and nine formerly Spanish-owned Matador AV-8Ss Sea Harriers. The Royal Thai Navy explained that the carrier would defend sea lanes, engage in search and rescue missions, and provide air support for Thai naval operations.

In June and July 1997, the Royal Thai Army reaffirmed to the U.S. government its wish to purchase 125 M60-A3 tanks from excess U.S. inventory, fitted with 105-mm guns and Tank Thermal Sight (TTS) capability. Also, official requests had been made to the U.S. government to purchase 37,500 M16-A2 rifles, 4,700 M4 carbines, 2,600 M203 grenade launchers, bayonets, and spare parts. In July, the Royal Thai Army was still inviting bids for the purchase of 295 armored vehicles (APCs), a purchase only later put on hold.

Therefore, in spite of the budget cuts and the economic difficulties, it was apparent that the armed forces were determined to continue to pursue modernization schemes, although at a lesser scale and slower pace. The immediate problem, however, was to pay for recently acquired or contracted hardware. With the baht at less than half its previous value and the purchases denominated in foreign currencies, the Thai military faced a tremendous payments burden.

It is expected that in 1998 alone, the Thai military will owe foreign arms suppliers approximately US$534 million, as part of the yearly installment payments.

Contributions to Regional and Global Security

REGIONAL SECURITY   Thai efforts to forge closer relations with the major powers as well as regional neighbors and to contain border disputes have helped reduce tensions and strengthen the region's security environment. Thailand's main contribution in 1997 came in the Cambodian crisis where, as noted above, it sheltered refugees. In addition, Thailand, Indonesia, and the Philippines served as ASEAN mediators, although without much success. Nevertheless, the role played by Thailand and its ASEAN counterparts helped maintain communications between the Cambodian factions and the outside world and perhaps limited the intensity of the fighting.

As an ASEAN member, Thailand supported the admission of Laos and Myanmar into ASEAN. It is an active although usually not leading member of the ASEAN Regional Forum (ARF) and the Asia-Pacific Economic Cooperation (APEC) forum. In ARF, Thailand served as a cochair of the Inter-Sessional Meeting on Disaster Relief. As the ASEAN coordinator for relations with the European Union, Thailand was particularly active in promoting closer ties between ASEAN and the EU, both within the ASEAN and Asia-Europe Meeting frameworks.

GLOBAL SECURITY   At the global level, Thailand's contributions mostly have come in multilateral fora. Thailand continued to be an active member of the Non-Aligned Movement (NAM) and worked closely with other developing countries on reform of the United Nations and UN peacekeeping operations. Thailand continued to serve, for the fourth consecutive year, as the NAM coordinator on UN peacekeeping operations. Thailand also served for the third consecutive year as the co-vice chair of the General Assembly open-ended working group on Security Council reform.

Despite its active role in the United Nations, Thailand continued to maintain only a token representation in the UN peacekeeping forces, with three military observers in the 1,174-member UN Iraq-Kuwait Observation Mission and three police officers in the 1,979-member UN Mission in Bosnia and Herzegovina.

August saw a major shift in the Royal Thai Army position on land mines when it announced its support for the campaign against land mines. Thailand subsequently became one of the original signatories to the land mine treaty. As a gesture of goodwill, the Royal Thai Army also announced that, within the next three years, it intends to complete the demining of the Thai-Cambodian border.

15 The United States

THE SECURITY ENVIRONMENT

Bill Clinton's second term as president of the United States began in January 1997. Through the first year of the second Clinton administration, the fundamental dilemmas of U.S. security policy remained how to define America's security interests and role following the removal of the Soviet threat at the beginning of the decade and how to maintain a credible and effective defense capability in the face of pressures to balance the budget and meet domestic priorities. Clinton's new national security team accepted the basic security assessments and policy frameworks developed by their predecessors between 1993 and 1996. No international events or new conceptual formulations appeared that crystallized the nature of the security challenge in what some were coming to call the "post post–cold war" period.

OFFICIAL ASSESSMENTS   The administration's view of the security environment was set out in two Congressionally mandated reports, both issued in May 1997. These were a presidential report on "A National Security Strategy for a New Century" and the Defense Department's "Quadrennial Defense Review," the fourth detailed review of American military forces and capabilities since the end of the cold war.

The National Security Strategy terms both the opportunities and the dangers of the new period "unprecedented." It cites opportunities for increased prosperity, an expanded democratic community, political stability, and the peaceful resolution of conflicts. The principal dangers are identified as ethnic conflict, "outlaw" states, terrorism, drugs, organized crime, and proliferation of weapons of mass destruction, plus the longer-term threats of environmental damage and population growth.

The Quadrennial Defense Review starts from the premise that the United States is now the world's leading military power and considers it unlikely that either a "global peer competitor" or a coalition of hostile states strong enough to challenge the United States would emerge between now and 2015 (the time horizon of the study). However, it says that the world nevertheless remains "a dangerous and highly uncertain place" and enumerates a series of possible threats to American interests and security. These include dangers of regional aggression by hostile or "failing" states, the proliferation of advanced weapons and technologies, "transnational" dangers including terrorism, drug traffic, and uncontrolled migration, as well as possible unconventional attacks on U.S. infrastructure, alliances, and political will.

Both reports ascribe major importance to the Asia Pacific region in U.S. national security calculations, virtually on a par with the continuing focus on Europe and the Eurasian region. The alliances with Japan and South Korea are seen as of key importance, and the Korean peninsula is viewed as the major flashpoint owing to North Korea's military capability, the unpredictability of the North Korean regime, and the current acute crisis in North Korea's economy. The National Security Strategy also cites the dynamic Southeast Asian subregion and U.S. alliances with members of the Association of Southeast Asian Nations (ASEAN) and Australia as important to U.S. strategic interests.

Both reports stress that the United States considers the role of China critical to regional stability and argue that the U.S. policy of engagement with China is the most effective strategy for encouraging China to be a responsible member of the regional community. However, the Quadrennial Defense Review also identifies China—along with Russia—as facing major economic and political uncertainties and as having the potential to emerge as a military competitor to the United States in the period beyond 2015. China's military modernization is described as a source of concern on the part of other countries in the region.

The U.S. Pacific Command's survey of regional security conditions also mentions China, North Korea, and Russia as possible sources of threat or instability. In addition, it cites competing claims in the South China Sea, the India-Pakistan dispute over Kashmir, internal insurgencies and unrest in Cambodia, Indonesia (East Timor), Myanmar, and Sri Lanka, and religious extremists in a number of countries as possible causes of conflict in the region.

U.S.–ASIA PACIFIC RELATIONS   China was in the spotlight in the United States throughout 1997, with the reversion of Hong Kong to Chinese control at the beginning of July and the state visit of President Jiang Zemin to the United States in October–November. Both events focused attention on the differences between those who emphasize the importance of not alienating China and favor an engagement approach, and those who give priority to human rights issues and advocate greater conditionality or sanctions against China. After initial emphasis on human rights and conditionality in its first term, the Clinton administration basically settled on the former approach, pursuing engagement on a broad agenda including the Korean situation, arms exports, and trade issues, while also addressing human rights questions without linking this to other subjects. The Jiang visit, despite blunt official exchanges on some questions and demonstrations by human rights activists at each of Jiang's stops, symbolized and appeared to solidify a more stable relationship—dubbed a "constructive strategic partnership"—at the highest level. Progress seemed to have been achieved on such questions as halting Chinese sales of advanced weapons to Iran.

It is worth noting that most U.S. critics of China do not portray Beijing as the new nemesis of the United States bent on world domination. Rather, they see China as a pariah state that violates basic human rights, oppresses Tibet, threatens to use force against Taiwan, exports advanced weapons to rogue states, and engages in unacceptable trade practices. Ironically, the U.S. security community is more conscious of the long-term potential for military conflict between the United States and China, and this group almost unanimously supports the engagement strategy.

The major event in U.S.-Japan security relations in 1997 was the issuance, on September 23, of revised Guidelines for U.S.-Japan Defense Cooperation, the culmination of an 18-month review process. The main import of the revised guidelines was to extend the range of circumstances under which Japan could actively support American security operations to include (unspecified) contingencies elsewhere in Asia Pacific. There was some controversy within Japan over whether the new guidelines were consistent with Japan's constitutional restrictions on the use of armed force.

China condemned the guidelines, claiming that they were being aimed at China. Efforts by both the U.S. and Japanese governments to convince Chinese leaders that the guidelines were not aimed at any specific country largely fell on deaf ears. Clearly, the principal object of Chinese concern was contingencies involving Taiwan, and although any Japanese government would face domestic political opposition to assisting the United States in a clash with China over Taiwan, no American and Japanese disclaimers based on the language of the guidelines could exclude this possibility. The guidelines themselves were the product of an effort to strengthen and focus attention on the positive aspects of U.S.-Japan security cooperation following a widely publicized campaign in Okinawa for the removal of the large U.S. force presence there, and it is questionable how carefully the possible Chinese reaction had been assessed before this process was launched.

Developments in the Korean peninsula underscored the volatility and complexity of the situation there. Painstaking negotiations proceeded through the year with North Korea over implementation of the agreement to provide two light water reactors as replacements for that country's existing reactors that were capable of producing material for nuclear weapons. Construction of the new reactors was ultimately begun, but the parallel steps toward inspection of the old reactors continued to meet resistance. Similar North Korean foot-dragging stalled efforts to organize talks on converting the 1953 armistice agreement into a permanent peace treaty, but the first session of the Four-Party Talks was finally held in Geneva in December. Also, catastrophic famine conditions led North Korea to accept international food contributions (from South Korea, the United States, and others) and even a degree of monitoring to ensure that supplies were not diverted to the military. The official accession of Kim Jong Il to his father's position as general secretary of the Korean Workers' Party during the year restored a degree of normalcy to the leadership structure but had little immediately apparent impact on decision-making.

The Southeast Asian financial crisis that began in Thailand in July and the heavy smoke from plantation and forest fires in Indonesia that inundated Malaysia and Singapore as well as parts of the Philippines in September and October provided dramatic demonstrations of the volatility of economic and environmental conditions and the dangers these can pose. In both cases, the United States was somewhat slow in formulating an active response. It declined to join an International Monetary Fund (IMF) program for Thailand put together in

August, and reacted unenthusiastically to proposals from Japan that a regional fund be established to help counter sudden exchange rate swings. However, in October the United States agreed to contribute US$3 billion to an IMF package for Indonesia, and in November the United States played a leading role in developing a framework agreement for handling future financial shocks that would include a regional financing arrangement to supplement the IMF. In response to the "haze" crisis, the U.S. government evacuated diplomatic dependents from Kuala Lumpur in September due to the health dangers, but contributed directly to countering the fire problem only in October when three military aircraft with water-dropping capability were dispatched to Indonesia. The United States also supported a Canadian initiative at the November Asia-Pacific Economic Cooperation meeting for closer cooperation among members in responding to natural disasters.

DIFFERENCES OVER PRIORITIES   The slow U.S. reaction to the Southeast Asian financial and environmental crises in part resulted from simple bureaucratic difficulties in dealing with new problems. However, as with policy toward China, it also reflected the continuing tug-of-war in U.S. international policy making between differing views of the international security environment, its significance for the United States, and policy priorities. Conflicting priorities also complicated other aspects of U.S. relations in Asia Pacific in 1997.

U.S. relations with Indonesia were affected by concerns within the White House over Congressional attitudes and domestic political issues. Prior to the 1996 election, the administration delayed notifying Congress of an agreed sale of fighter aircraft to Indonesia. It was feared that notification would trigger renewed Congressional criticisms of Indonesia over East Timor and human rights, plus more publicity on a scandal involving illegal fund-raising by an Indonesian-born Democratic campaign official. Further delays in notification in 1997, coupled with further sharp criticism by some members of Congress, led Indonesian President Suharto in June to pull out of the aircraft deal, and also to withdraw from a modest but useful U.S. military education program.

U.S. policy toward Myanmar continued to be driven by human rights concerns. In mid-1997, the Clinton administration placed new restrictions on U.S. investment in Myanmar, as a means of demonstrating these concerns. The United States also opposed the ASEAN governments' decision in July to admit Myanmar into the expanded ASEAN. In contrast to its approach with China, regarding Myanmar the United States gave priority to issues of civil and political rights, whereas the ASEAN governments pursued a longer-term strategy of engagement aimed ultimately at solidifying a Southeast Asia–wide grouping.

Defense Policies and Issues

ENGAGEMENT   The May 1997 National Security Strategy report reiterated the basic objectives of the Clinton administration's strategy in similar terms to the formulation in its first-term "engagement and enlargement" policy. The stated objectives are (1) to enhance security with effective diplomacy and with military forces that are ready to fight and win; (2) to bolster America's economic prosperity; and (3) to promote democracy abroad. The new formulation is somewhat broader and more general than the earlier version, which did not mention diplomacy as a major instrument of national security policy and which stressed both increasing U.S. economic competitiveness and enlarging the world of "compatible political and economic systems." However, the new formulation still does not provide clear guidance on setting priorities among the objectives.

Another continuing dilemma for U.S. security policy is resources. The combination of five years of concerted federal budget cutting and a sustained seven-year economic expansion reduced the estimated budget deficit for 1997 to US$22 billion, one-tenth of its level in 1992. However, much of the cuts came from the defense budget. Defense spending dropped from 6.5 percent of gross national product in 1985 to 4 percent by 1995 and an estimated 3.2 percent in 1997, representing a decline in real terms of 38 percent over the 12-year period. The Quadrennial Defense Review projects that the budget is likely to remain at roughly $250 billion for the foreseeable future, and may even decline further unless there is a deterioration in the international security environment.

Correspondingly, the number of U.S. military personnel fell by 32 percent, from 2.13 million on active duty in fiscal year 1989 to 1.45 million in fiscal 1997. The number of active army divisions was cut from 16 to 10, air force fighter wings from 22 to 13, and the 600-ship navy planned in the Reagan administration fell to around 430.

The procurement portion of the defense budget—the development and acquisition of equipment and weapons systems—dropped even more sharply, falling by 63 percent in real terms from 1985 to US$44 billion in 1997. To reach the US$60 billion level it sees as the minimum needed to acquire the technology and systems to sustain American military superiority, the Quadrennial Defense Review recommends further reductions in personnel strength and force structure, plus two additional rounds of base closures.

Procurement and base questions affect communities and businesses throughout the country, so defense budgets are subject to intense scrutiny and adjustment by the Congress. In 1997 as in 1996, Congress appropriated more funds for defense than the president had requested. Congress also must approve a special procedure for each round of base closures in advance, and after several rounds of often painful closures in recent years, opposition to further cuts is likely to be strong. Thus both the amount and the allocation of future defense spending remain difficult to predict with any precision.

Contributions to Global and Regional Security

GLOBAL   The United States plays a major role in global security, but there is a continuing debate within American society as to what the U.S. global role should be. The Quadrennial Defense Review describes two "competing visions" of the U.S. role. One is the isolationist argument that America should focus its energies on domestic problems and only become involved in international conflicts when U.S. survival is threatened. The other view is that, as the only remaining superpower, the United States has an obligation to play the role of world police officer. Both of these formulations are exaggerated, but elements of the arguments can be heard in public and Congressional debate over most international security issues.

The Quadrennial Defense Review argues that American global interests are best served by a middle ground "strategy of engagement" featuring the *selective* use of U.S. forces, as part of a coalition of allies and other like-minded states where possible. This is the fundamental approach of the Clinton administration, as of the previous Bush administration, and it has ultimately won public and Congressional support—though sometimes after extended debate—in most of the specific situations that have arisen to date in the post–cold war period. Burden-sharing, both in participation and in financing, remains a major factor affecting public and Congressional attitudes toward U.S. international military activities.

FORWARD DEPLOYMENT   Both the 1997 National Security Strategy and the Quadrennial Defense Review endorse the U.S. forward military presence in Asia Pacific. In support of the fundamental policy of maintaining the capability to fight and win major conflicts in two different regions "nearly simultaneously," administration policy is to maintain "roughly 100,000 military personnel" deployed in both Europe and the Asia Pacific region. (These figures reflect significant reductions in the 1990s, especially in Europe.) Repeated statements by high-level U.S. officials have elevated the 100,000 figure to the status of a firm numerical commitment.

The Quadrennial Defense Review reconciles its recommendations for cuts in military manpower with its support for maintaining present overseas troop levels by assuming that in a two-conflict situation some specialized units, such as bombers and amphibious assault forces, would be able to "swing" between the theaters. However, in his comments on the Quadrennial Defense Review, the chairman of the joint chiefs of staff registered concern over the stress on personnel of the existing high level of operations, and the potential impact of the further force cuts. Further, an independent panel established by the Congress to review the Quadrennial Defense Review in a year-end report questioned the review's emphasis on fighting a two-theater traditional conflict, and urged that the military focus instead on the force structures necessary to counter new threats, such as attacks by "rogue" states armed with weapons of mass destruction. In Asia Pacific, a resolution of the confrontation on the Korean peninsula would also likely lead to pressures (in both countries) to reduce the 35,000 American troops now stationed in South Korea.

Thus it cannot be expected that the 100,000 troop commitment will remain immutable as security assessments and conditions in the region continue to evolve. However, in practice moderate reductions in the numbers of troops in the region need not materially reduce the U.S. ability to project power into the region.

BILATERAL DIALOGUES   The U.S. forward military presence in Asia Pacific is part of a network of bilateral defense alliances, relationships, and dialogues. The maintenance of this network requires intense dialogue between the United States and its regional partners—particularly major allies Japan, South Korea, and Australia, but also including the Philippines and Thailand and other nonallied but friendly governments as well. Negotiations over operational questions such as troop presence or logistical support are complex and can touch sensitive domestic political nerves in the partner country. The perennial controversy in Japan over the large U.S. presence in that country, particularly in Okinawa, and the delicate discussions of these subjects between the two governments is an example of the sensitivities of these dialogues.

The United States also attempts to develop constructive dialogues with countries with which U.S. relations have been strained or conflictual, in order to manage the conflicts and move toward the resolution of issues. China and North Korea—and Vietnam—fall into this category. Both the Chinese and North Korean relationships remain difficult, as illustrated by the mixed reception that Jiang received on his state visit to the United States and the many stops and starts in the negotiations with North Korea over nuclear and other issues. Moves toward accommodation also invariably evoke some domestic criticism, but the Clinton administration has persisted in these dialogues, and absent major crises or breaches of faith it can be expected to continue to do so.

MULTILATERAL SECURITY DIALOGUES The administration has also maintained its policy set down in 1993 of actively supporting the developing institutions and processes for multilateral dialogues in the Asia Pacific region. The attendance of Secretary of State Madeleine Albright at the 1997 ASEAN Post-Ministerial Conferences and the ASEAN Regional Forum security dialogue meeting in Kuala Lumpur in July, where she urged the ASEAN states to take common action in response to the Hun Sen coup in Cambodia, was one clear illustration of this policy. There are limited short-term expectations from these dialogues, but they are seen as an important long-term undertaking.

The establishment of a Northeast Asia forum as the counterpart to ASEAN in Southeast Asia continues to be favored by American officials, especially as a supporting mechanism for efforts to resolve the Korean stalemate. Following the issuance of the revised Guidelines for U.S.-Japan Defense Cooperation in September 1997, and in reaction to China's criticism of the guidelines, proposals were floated—primarily in Japan—for a tripartite China-Japan-U.S. dialogue. The

Clinton administration indicated it would welcome such a dialogue, although China appears to be reluctant to participate.

The United States also endorses a number of other dialogue processes in the region in which the country is not directly involved. These include the ASEAN-sponsored talks on the South China Sea and discussions of territorial and other issues involving China and Taiwan, Russia and Japan, Russia and China, and India and Pakistan. The China-Taiwan dialogue is the most sensitive of these for the United States, whose recognition of the People's Republic of China as the government of all China has always been coupled with insistence that China not attempt to reintegrate Taiwan by force. The United States was encouraged at signs of a thaw in the long stalemate between Russia and Japan over the Northern Territories issue at the informal bilateral summit in late 1997, and welcomed the Sino-Russian agreement on the location of their long common border and on a reduced troop presence in the border areas. (The United States would be less comfortable over indications of a resumed strategic relationship between China and Russia, but the 1997 agreements did not appear aimed in this direction.) Finally, American officials played an active role in encouraging renewed talks between India and Pakistan.

16 Vietnam

The Security Environment

Vietnamese view security in comprehensive terms. Security is not simply a matter of protecting sovereignty and territorial integrity, although these are essential elements. It also embraces protection of national political, economic, and social systems and the physical environment. Moreover, in many of these areas national security is inseparable from regional and even global security and cannot be achieved except in cooperation with other countries. The Vietnamese comprehensive security concept must be viewed in the historical context of Vietnam's very painful and prolonged struggle to regain independence. This has led to a domestic emphasis on economic renovation as laid out in the sixth National Party Congress in 1986 and on strengthening Vietnam's bilateral and regional relations to provide a peaceful, supportive environment for economic renovation.

DOMESTIC SECURITY   Domestically, 1997 was a year of important transitions. Vietnam's top leaders, Do Muoi, general secretary of the Central Committee of the Communist Party of Vietnam, President Le Duc Anh, and Prime Minister Vo Van Kiet, did not seek reelection to the National Assembly in the July elections. At the end of the year, Le Kha Phieu, a former general, assumed the position of party general secretary. This transition went smoothly and the basic policy direction was affirmed by the new leadership. The newly elected National Assembly membership is younger and better educated. Fully one-third of the members are now women, of whom four hold ministerial rank.

Domestic security policy during 1997 centered on three national economic programs in the fields of food production, export processing, and consumer goods production. Despite significant progress from a low base, many challenges to comprehensive security exist in the form of high unemployment, gender and urban/rural inequities, and unmet needs in education, environmental safeguards, and income standards. Other challenges include corruption, prostitution, drug abuse, trafficking in women, weakened family ethics, and tax evasion. Vietnamese believe that true security requires the effective punishment of criminals regardless of their social rank.

EXTERNAL SECURITY   From Vietnam's perspective, the Asia Pacific region appears relatively stable, in line with the general worldwide trend toward increased peace, stability, and development cooperation. There remain many uncertainties, however, including the possibility of new domestic and external conflicts based on conflicts of resources or national, ethnic, and religious contradictions. Global problems such as environmental destruction, transnational crime, and drug trafficking are becoming increasingly salient.

The improved relations among the larger powers during 1997 positively benefited the external security environment, but the financial crisis affecting most of the countries of Southeast Asia created new security challenges. According to the General Statistics Department, trade with the member countries of the Association of Southeast Asian Nations (ASEAN) dropped 8 percent in 1997 compared with the preceding year, and inward direct foreign investment fell 63 percent. To cope with the crisis and maintain its economic development program, Vietnam established a surveillance mechanism for financial and monetary transactions. The efforts of international organizations such as the International Monetary Fund, the World Bank, and the Asian Development Bank to deal with the crisis and restore confidence were much appreciated in Vietnam.

Relations with Southeast Asian Neighbors. Vietnam's more immediate environment has been marked by its successful efforts to strengthen relations with neighboring powers. Notable developments included:
- Numerous measures to upgrade Vietnamese-Laotian cooperation. Regular high-level official meetings and summit visits took place on the 20th anniversary of the Vietnam-Laos Treaty of Friendship and Cooperation. Despite wide-ranging cooperation

in the cultural, scientific, environmental, communication, transport, and other fields, the two countries still need to strengthen their efforts to prevent illegal border crossings and drug trafficking.
- Vietnam's continued respect for Cambodia's independence, sovereignty, and sanctity of domestic affairs during the political crisis in that country. Vietnam welcomed the proposal made by First Cambodian Prime Minister Ung Huot to resume negotiations on border issues. Because of uncertainties in Cambodia prior to the 1998 elections, Vietnam continues to need to cooperate with Cambodian efforts to maintain Cambodian security and social stability and to prevent illegal border smuggling.
- Maritime cooperation with other Southeast Asian nations. The Thai-Vietnam border demarcation agreement was the first such accord signed by Vietnam in conformity with international law and practice, and Vietnam hopes to resolve border issues with its other neighbors in a similar way. Vietnam is also preparing its second mission to Indonesia to propose a similar border demarcation agreement. With Malaysia, Vietnam has started joint exploration of petroleum in overlapping claims; with the Philippines, it is engaged in maritime research.

Relations with Large Powers. Vietnam is enjoying normalized relations with China and is bolstering its friendly relations with that country and its cooperation in many fields. There are annual Sino-Vietnamese summit meetings. In July 1997, Do Muoi visited China, and this was followed by trips by a number of other high-ranking officials. Concrete agreements cover the economy, trade, cooperation in science and technology, and educational ties. The two countries have agreed to open the Kunming-Haiphong railway and have signed a protocol on road cooperation.

One concrete result of Do Muoi's trip was an agreement with Chinese President Jiang Zemin to reach a border agreement on land and Tonkin Gulf sea border demarcation by the year 2000. While much progress has been made on the land border, the respective Chinese and Vietnamese proposals show considerable variance on the maritime boundaries. China refused to discuss the Paracel Islands and continued to claim the Spratlys. It regards a considerable part of Vietnam's continental shelf and exclusive economic zone as Chinese. Negotiations are continuing.

Vietnam's relations with Russia entered a new stage. Prime Minister

Viktor Chernomyrdin visited Vietnam on November 24–26, 1997, the first visit by a Russian prime minister since the disintegration of the Soviet Union. The two sides signed a number of agreements embodying economic, scientific, and cultural cooperation, restoring traditional friendship on the basis of mutual respect, benefit, and equality.

Japanese Prime Minister Hashimoto Ryutaro's visit to Vietnam in January 1997 symbolized the support that Japan is giving for Vietnam's development. Japan is the country's largest trade partner and biggest bilateral aid donor.

There were also positive developments in Vietnam's relations with the United States. The two countries have exchanged ambassadors, established consulates-general in Ho Chi Minh City and San Francisco, and normalized their diplomatic relations. They have agreed to settle debt issues and work toward signing a trade agreement normalizing their economic ties. Four rounds of talks have taken place on this subject, and Vietnam hopes to receive normal (most favored nation) trade treatment from the United States during 1998.

Despite an overall improvement in the security environment, Vietnam's sovereign rights over its water in the Eastern Sea remain threatened.

Defense Policy and Issues

Vietnam's national defense is peaceful and emphasizes self-defense aimed at ensuring its national interests, independence, and full sovereignty and the territorial integration of Vietnam. Defense is based on the concept of the entire people's national defense. Diplomacy also serves the interest of defense. The Vietnamese government is willing to conduct peaceful negotiations with all countries to settle historical or emerging problems, including the countries with which it has maritime disputes.

Some principles of Vietnamese defense policy include:
- Vietnam will not engage in disputes or wars outside the country, nor will it participate in any military alliance or operation that is counter to safeguarding peace. It does not engage in military deterrence nor employ the threat of force.
- Vietnam engages in preventive defense, drawing back from the dangers of war. It supports non-nuclear policies and opposes the proliferation of nuclear or other weapons of mass destruction.

- Vietnam's defense policy opposes military occupation or the sending of troops abroad or the building of foreign military bases.

Vietnam, for the first time in its history, is working on a defense white paper. In the past, defense affairs were regarded as secret, but Vietnam now sees some level of transparency as essential to building a more peaceful world. The third draft of the white paper was finished in 1997 and is now being considered for approval.

Vietnam's armed forces not only defend its national land territory but also safeguard a 3,200-mile coastline and large territorial waters and air space. Given its underdeveloped economy and strictly defense-oriented policies, Vietnam neither wants nor can afford to engage in an arms race. However, there is a consensus that like other Asia Pacific countries, Vietnam should reduce troop numbers to a level compatible with its economic resources but essential to its mission. Vietnam must attach utmost importance to raising the professional quality and fighting capacity of its armed forces and making appropriate investments in military manpower and hardware.

Contributions to Regional and Global Security

Vietnam's eighth National Party Congress in 1996 called for promotion of Vietnam's foreign relations with other countries. The successful efforts in this regard are one of the achievements of the "Doi Moi" (renovation) policy of the past decade. Vietnam now has normalized relations with all the major powers, established diplomatic relations with 163 countries, and entered many international and regional organizations, most especially ASEAN. This gives it a strong base for a more active international role, although given its current economic status, Vietnam's highest priority and main contribution to regional and global order lies in strengthening its own economy and society.

Vietnam joined ASEAN in 1995, and although the country is a new member of ASEAN, it has adapted itself quickly to the organization and contributed to many ASEAN activities. As part of its overall effort to integrate itself into the regional and global economies, Vietnam joined the ASEAN Free Trade Area (AFTA) in 1995 and is striving to fulfill its commitments in implementing AFTA. The government has approved a timetable to reduce tariffs of most imported goods by 2006. Vietnam is also participating in negotiations to establish an ASEAN Investment Area. In 1997, Vietnam favored the expansion of

ASEAN to include Myanmar as well as Laos, opposing Western pressures against Myanmar's admission. It also supports the early admission of Cambodia.

Vietnam will host the 1998 ASEAN summit. At the November 1997 Vancouver Leaders' Meeting of the Asia-Pacific Economic Cooperation forum, Vietnam was one of three countries accepted as new members, and it will formally join the organization in 1998. Vietnamese organizations participate actively in both the ASEAN Regional Forum and in the track two Council for Security Cooperation in Asia Pacific. As previously referred to, the Vietnamese people now believe that dialogues and transparency through such multilateral governmental and nongovernmental fora are conducive to building regional and global peace and prosperity.

Vietnam is playing a leading role in the Francophone Conference, involving 49 countries and territories with a population of about 500 million. In 1997, Vietnam hosted the seventh Francophone Conference and successfully proposed to strengthen the conference by making economic cooperation an explicit goal. The conference demonstrated Vietnam's ability to assume international leadership and provided Vietnam with needed experience for hosting the 1998 ASEAN summit conference.

Vietnam regards the United Nations as an essential tool for international understanding and relations. In 1997, it was elected a member of the UN Economic and Social Council and became vice-chair of the 52nd General Assembly.

The APSO Project Team

A distinctive feature of the *Asia Pacific Security Outlook* is that it is based on background papers developed by analysts from the region. These analysts, many of them younger specialists, meet at an annual workshop to examine each country paper and discuss the overall regional outlook. They also fill out a questionnaire, which is used to develop the regional overview and provide an assessment of changing perceptions over time.

Those involved in the process of developing the 1998 *Asia Pacific Security Outlook* include the following people.

COUNTRY ANALYSTS
(BACKGROUND PAPER WRITER IDENTIFIED BY AN ASTERISK)

AUSTRALIA   Andrew Mack, Australian National University*
CANADA   Brian L. Job, University of British Columbia*
CHINA   Chu Shulong, China Institute of Contemporary International Relations*
EUROPEAN UNION   Hanns Maull, University of Trier*
INDONESIA   Kusnanto Anggoro, Centre for Strategic and International Studies*
JAPAN   Katahara Eiichi, Kobe Gakuin University*
REPUBLIC OF KOREA   Lee Jung-Hoon, Yonsei University; Song Young-sun, Korea Institute of Defense Analysis*
MALAYSIA   Abdul Razak Abdullah Baginda, Malaysia Centre for Strategic Studies*; Mely Caballero-Anthony, Institute of Strategic and International Studies*; Mohamed Jawhar bin Hassan, Institute of Strategic and International Studies
NEW ZEALAND   David Dickens, Centre for Strategic Studies, Victoria University of Wellington*
PAPUA NEW GUINEA   Ronald May, Australian National University*; Henry Ivarature, National Research Institute*
PHILIPPINES   Gina Pattugalan, University of the Philippines*

RUSSIA   Dmitri Trenin, Carnegie Moscow Center, Carnegie Endowment for International Peace*; Ivan S. Tselichtchev, Niigata University of Management
SINGAPORE   Kwa Chong Guan, Singapore Institute of International Affairs*
THAILAND   Darmp Sukontasap, Chulalongkorn University*
UNITED STATES   Richard W. Baker, East-West Center*
VIETNAM   Pham Thi Lan Phuong, Institute of International Relations*

EDITOR/OVERVIEW   Charles E. Morrison, Director, APEC Study Center, East-West Center

PROJECT DIRECTORS   Charles E. Morrison; Nishihara Masashi, Professor of International Relations, National Defense Academy; and Jusuf Wanandi, Chairman of the Supervisory Board, Centre for Strategic and International Studies

STAFF SUPPORT

Furuya Ryota, Program Assistant, Japan Center for International Exchange
Kawaguchi Chie, Editorial Researcher, Japan Center for International Exchange
Marilu Khudari, Secretary, East-West Center
Koizumi Hiroko, Keyboarder, Japan Center for International Exchange
Kumai Mariko, Program Assistant, Japan Center for International Exchange
Noda Makito, Chief Program Officer and Director for Research Coordination, Japan Center for International Exchange
Pamela J. Noda, Editor, Japan Center for International Exchange
Wada Shuichi, Program Officer, Japan Center for International Exchange
Yamakawa Kyoko, Program Assistant, Japan Center for International Exchange

Asia Pacific Security Outlook 1997 can be ordered from the East-West Center, 1601 East-West Road, Honolulu, Hawaii 96848-1601 U.S.A.

The Asia Pacific Agenda Project

The Asia Pacific Agenda Project (APAP) was established in November 1995 to enhance policy-oriented intellectual exchange at the nongovernmental level, with special emphasis on independent research institutions in the region. It consists of four interconnected components: (1) the Asia Pacific Agenda Forum, a gathering of leaders of Asia Pacific policy research institutes to explore the future agenda for collaborative research and dialogue activities related to the development of an Asia Pacific community; (2) an Asia Pacific policy research information network utilizing the Internet; (3) annual multilateral joint research projects on pertinent issues of regional and global importance undertaken in collaboration with major research institutions in the region; and (4) collaborative research activities designed to nurture a new generation of Asia Pacific leaders who can participate in international intellectual dialogues. APAP is managed by an international steering committee composed of nine major research institutions in the region. The Japan Center for International Exchange has served as secretariat since APAP's inception.

The Japan Center for International Exchange

Founded in 1970, the Japan Center for International Exchange (JCIE) is an independent, nonprofit, and nonpartisan organization dedicated to strengthening Japan's role in international affairs. JCIE believes that Japan faces a major challenge in augmenting its positive contributions to the international community, in keeping with its position as one of the world's largest industrial democracies. Operating in a country where policy-making has traditionally been dominated by the government bureaucracy, JCIE has played an important role in broadening debate on Japan's international responsibilities by conducting international and cross-sectional programs of exchange, research, and discussion.

JCIE creates opportunities for informed policy discussions; it does not take policy positions. JCIE programs are carried out with the collaboration and cosponsorship of many organizations. The contacts developed through these working relationships are crucial to JCIE's efforts to increase the number of Japanese from the private sector engaged in meaningful policy research and dialogue with overseas counterparts.

JCIE receives no government subsidies; rather, funding comes from private foundation grants, corporate contributions, and contracts.

Other JCIE Books on Asia Pacific

China-Japan-U.S.: Managing the Trilateral Relationship, by Morton I. Abramowitz, Funabashi Yoichi, and Wang Jisi

Challenges for China-Japan-U.S. Cooperation, edited by Kokubun Ryosei

Emerging Civil Society in the Asia Pacific Community, edited by Tadashi Yamamoto

An Emerging China in a World of Interdependence (The Triangle Papers: 45), by Yoichi Funabashi, Michel Oksenberg, and Heinrich Weiss

Managing the International System over the Next Ten Years: Three Essays (The Triangle Papers: 50), by Bill Emmott, Koji Watanabe, and Paul Wolfowitz

Community Building with Pacific Asia (The Triangle Papers: 51), by Charles E. Morrison, Akira Kojima, and Hanns W. Maull

The New Research Agenda in Asia Pacific: Bali Forum January 11–12, 1997 (The JCIE Papers: 20)

The Rationale and Common Agenda for Asia-Europe Cooperation CAEC Task Force Reports, Council for Asia-Europe Cooperation

Outside Japan, please order *China-Japan-U.S.* and *Challenges for China-Japan-U.S. Cooperation* from The Brookings Institution, Dept. 029, Washington, D.C. 20042-0029 U.S.A. (Fax: 202-797-6004). Within Japan and for other titles, please request ordering information from the Japan Center for International Exchange, 9-7 Minami Azabu 4-chome, Minato-ku, Tokyo 106-0047, Japan (Fax: 03-3443-7580; e-mail: admin@jcie.or.jp).